MARSILIO CLASSICS

Luigi Ballerini and Andrew Wood, Editors

THE COFFEE HOUSE

A Comedy in Three Acts
Bilingual Edition

Carlo Goldoni
The Coffee House

translated by Jeremy Parzen
introduction by Franco Fido

MARSILIO PUBLISHERS
NEW YORK

This Book is Part of the Marsilio Classics Series
Luigi Ballerini and Andrew Wood, Editors

Original Italian Title: *La bottega del caffè*

Translation Copyright © 1998
Marsilio Publishers, New York

Introduction Copyright © 1998
Franco Fido

Printed in the United States of America
ISBN 0-941419-85-1
LOC 92-62368

Library of Congress Cataloging-in-Publication Data

Goldoni, Carlo, 1707-1793
  [Bottega del caffè. English]
  The coffee house / Carlo Goldoni ; translated by Jeremy Parzen ;
introduction by Franco Fido.
      p.   cm. — (Marsilio classics)
  Includes bibliographical references.
  ISBN 0-941419-85-1 (pbk. ; alk. paper)
  I. Parzen, Jeremy. II. Title. III. Series.
PQ4695.E5B6   1998
852' .6—dc21
                                                    98-41650
                                                      CIP

Marsilio Publishers wishes to thank Professor Nicolas Perrella and the Gladys Krieble Delmas Foundation for its generous support of The Goldoni Edition Project

CONTENTS

INTRODUCTION
by Franco Fido

1750-51 [handwritten]

I.

La bottega del caffè (*The Coffee House*) is one of the sixteen comedies that Carlo Goldoni wrote and had staged in 1750-51, keeping a promise he had made the year before to his Venetian public in order to persuade them to remain faithful to the Sant'Angelo Theater, for which he was working. Since 1748, the year of his return from Pisa (where he had carried on legal practice), Goldoni was bound by contract, as "theatrical poet," to the Medebach Company, with the obligation to provide the actors with a number of plays each year for five years—there will be about fifty, by the end of the contract. This was, from 1748 to 1753, the moment of the so-called reform of the theater, which implied the replacement of the elementary and often scurrilous scenarios of the heavily improvised Commedia dell'Arte by fully-scripted comedies. In these latter, characters taken from real life merchants, impoverished noblemen, gondoliers, craftsmen speaking colorful everyday language—Italian or Venetian according to their status—went through plausible and amusing adventures, tied together in a credible plot and happily ending with the reward of virtue and punishment of vice.

In both form and substance, *The Coffee House* is meant to conform to this model. Around the tables of the honest coffeehouse keeper, Ridolfo, several customers meet regularly: Eugenio, a young merchant who neglects his wife and is running heavily into debt due to a passion for gambling; Pandolfo, the owner of the gaming house, and Leandro, the cardsharp, who together take advantage of Eugenio's vice and are ruining him; a mysterious wayfarer who, it will be discovered in due time, is Leandro's abandoned wife, having arrived from Turin in search of her husband; and Eugenio's wife, Vittoria, who, availing herself of the Carnival freedom, comes masked to the coffee house in search of her profligate spouse. Among these characters the most remarkable patron of *The Coffee House* is Don Marzio, a Neapolitan nobleman with little money and no occupation, who by gossiping spreads suspicions and causes mishaps. In the end, it will be his chattering with a stranger—a police sergeant in fact—that unmasks the cheating Pandolfo and makes his arrest possible.

These are commonplace events and inconsequential vicissitudes, made concrete and significant however, by the city life reflected in the "day" of the coffee house: "At this hour travelers, workmen, boatmen, and sailors come, all the people who rise with the dawn" (I, p. 9). It is precisely the brilliant placement of the action in a coffee shop that first must draw our attention.

II.

As we know, in the eighteenth century, coffee houses were popular and versatile establishments, whose greater or lesser respectability stretched on a wide range. At the lowest level we might find the Caffè degli Italiani in London, where shady adventurers used to meet, and away from which the knowledgeable Casanova advised Da Ponte to remain.[1] A little "above" this are the coffee houses of Paris described with precision and zest by Sébastien Mercier:

> There are [in Paris] six to seven hundred cafés: they are the ordinary refuge of idlers, and the shelter of the poor, who keep warm there in wintertime, to spare firewood at home. Some of these coffee houses are like academic bureaus, in which authors and plays are judged [. . .]. Some fellows arrive there around ten o'clock in the morning, and they do not leave before eleven at night [. . .]. It isn't decent to linger on at the café, as that shows a penury of knowledge, and a total want of social connections. Nevertheless, a coffee house where learned and distinguished people would convene would be preferable,

because of its liberty and gaiety, to all our clubs, that are sometimes quite boring. . . .[2]

More or less of the same kind were the London coffee houses that we find mentioned in the *Spectator*: those in the neighbourhood of the Law Courts where contentious students debated politics (in issue 197), or religion (issue 476), or else those, from Charing-Cross to Covent-Garden, where the most impudent liars used to tell a thousand fibs (issue 521). But in English coffee houses one could also find well-read and well-mannered patrons, like the readers of Boileau, Corneille and Racine noticed by the same Addison at *Will's* during a memorable exploration of the major cafés in the capital undertaken to gather popular reactions to the death of Louis XIV in 1715 (issue 403).[3]

More intellectual were certain coffee houses in Paris, such as the *Procope*, where, as Montesquieu jokingly says, "they make coffee in such a way, that it gives wit to all those who drink it: or at least there isn't anyone, among those who leave the house, who is not convinced that he is four times wittier than when he came in";[4] or the *Régence*, meeting place for the strongest chess players in town, and theater of the immortal dialogue between Diderot and the Neveu de Rameau.

The coffee houses praised by Gasparo Gozzi in his magazine *L'Osservatore* seem equally worth admiring ("You would believe that you are looking not at a shop, but at some delicious theatrical show, with many beautiful sights [. . .] After frequenting a café for six months, a honest man will go out into the world with all the learning he is inclined to absorb."),[5] or the Milanese coffee house imagined by Pietro Verri, where he

who wants to read finds at his disposal the *Giornale enciclopedico* and the *Estratto della letteratura europea* and such good reviews of interesting news, thanks to which men, who used to be Roman, Florentine, Genoese or Lombard, now are practically European; in that shop there is a good atlas, that helps to settle questions arising from political news: in that shop, finally, different people gather, some reasonable, some unreasonable, who talk, joke, or take things seriously . . .[6]

III.

All these types of coffee houses, from the most ill-famed to the most reputable, seem to find a place—like so many other phenomena and institutions of the contemporary world—in the vast landscape of Goldoni's theater: from the short libretto or *intermezzo*, *La bottega de caffè* (1736), to the present comedy, *Bottega del caffè* (1750), through many others including *Il contrattempo* (*The Hitch*, 1753), *Il festino* (*The Dancing Party*) and *Il filosofo inglese* (*The English Philosopher*, 1754), *Le morbinose* (*The Merry Women*, 1758), *Le avventure della villeggiatura* (*Adventures in the Country*, 1761), *Il matrimonio per concorso* (*The Marriage by Contest*, 1763), *Il ventaglio* (*The Fan*, 1765).

Generally, in the later texts the coffee house functions to allow people to meet in the open and chat or read. But in the early intermezzo version, in our *Coffee House* and to a certain extent in *The English Philosopher* the setting plays a more central and complex role.

In the 1736 *intermezzo*, *Coffee House*, a Venetian coffee shop owner called Narciso and a pretty Roman adventuress join forces to fleece Zanetto, a rather chickenhearted young man of good family. When they have stripped him of all his money and jewels, they scare him away with the sudden apparition of a mustachioed bully (the very same Narciso in disguise) and marry: a marriage that promises to be an effective association to swindle future patrons of the house. The *foglietti* or "little papers" from London and Madrid that the ignorant Zanetto tries to decipher, making a lot of ridiculous blunders, in Narciso's shop, are much more at home in the opening scene of *The English Philosopher*. There, the owner of a book shop that occupies one half of the background, sends them to the owner of the coffee house visible on the other half:

BIRONE (clerk of the bookseller)
> Here are the papers that my boss is sending yours,
> The usual newspapers from Paris and Holland,
> The *Mercure Galant* of which they talk so much,
> And the current issue of our own *Spectator*.

GIOACCHINO (waiter of the coffee house)
> Oh yes, the curious readers will feast in them.
> Of news the idle critics will get a bellyful;
> Without a bit of sense, without any discretion,
> Each of them will be heard to utter his opinion.

To be sure this coffee house, in a Goldonian London teeming with true and false philosophers, foreigners and craftsmen, resembles those described forty years earlier by Addison in the real *Spectator*.

At an equal distance, one could say, from the coffee house of Narciso and the one patronized by the English philosopher, stands Ridolfo's *bottega* in the 1750 comedy we now have before us. Goldoni himself stresses the importance for the play's action in his *Mémoires*:

> I do not point in the title of this play to a story, a passion, a character; but to a coffee house, where several actions unfold at the same time, where several persons are led by different interests; and if I succeeded in establishing an essential relationship between these various objects, and in rendering them necessary to each other, I believe that I fulfilled my duty . . .[7]

IV.

On their part, recent critics have pointed out the sharp contrast between the characters of the various plays. In the *intermezzo*, to overcome the risks of his trade, the vicious Narciso turns his shop into a gaming den and *maison de rendez vous*; while the comedy's upright Ridolfo has just inherited the profession of coffee house keeper, the more doubtful activities are carried on in the *Bottega del caffè* by Pandolfo, the owner of the gambling house. We could add that the assonance of the names, Ridolfo, Pandolfo further suggests a splitting into two halves, one all good, the other all bad, similar to that doubling later invented by Italo Calvino in his *Visconte dimezzato*.

Thus Goldoni, who at the end of the play rewards Ridolfo and punishes Pandolfo by having him arrested and jailed, ignores in the 1750 comedy those dangerous fluctuations in the coffee market that fifteen years earlier had conditioned Narciso's professional outlook in the *intermezzo*. In order to emphasize, on the stage of the Sant'Angelo, *les prospéités de la vertu* (to paraphrase Sade), and pursue the moralistic goals of his reform.[8] Another contrast, within the comedy, is that between the thrust towards adventurous and unruly actions coming from the Commedia dell'Arte (its conventions having yet to be fully shaken off), and a fixed, recognizably Venetian space, which—again in accordance with the reform—should make the story more consistent and "realistic."[9]

The interpretations advanced in two essays of the special issue that the American review *Annali D'Italianistica* devoted to Goldoni on the bicentennial of his death are more ambitious than simply noting these internal and external contrasts. Ilaria Crotti underlines the symbiosis, in the 1736 *intermezzo*, between theater and coffee house, the latter being like the former "a place of masks and disguises"; and mustering a lavish display of authorities and citations (from Bachtin to Camporesi, from Fontana and Fournel to Mauzi, from Paul Hazard to Habermas) she discovers both in the 1750 *Coffee House* and in the *English Philosopher*, "an explicit and programmatic search for a drama-turgic rendition of the forms in which the *opinion publique* and its confused humming get organized," as if Goldoni's coffee shops were the *Procope* of the Parisian *philosophes*, or the *Orange Coffee House* where distinguished foreigners gathered in London. Ridolfo's modest establishment surprisingly becomes "a place for listening and for storytelling, for life and for its transposition—that excludes the negative pulsions still implicit in the *intermezzo*—to shine in its exemplarity." At the same time and no less surprisingly, in this confident cosmopolitan perspective Narciso and Ridolfo end by resembling each other: "We see then that Ridolfo is [. . .] the direct heir of the earlier coffee house owner, in the sense that he reveals, scene after scene, that same vocation for stage-directing and ability to organize the others' voices [. . .] that the former [Narcisco] had already shown."[10]

Jackson Cope also speaks of Ridolfo as a "stage-director," and as a man far less virtuous than he claims to be (and so more similar to either Narciso, or even Pandolfo). In Cope's subtle, "neo-Elisabethan" (or at least neo-gothic) reading, *The Coffee House* becomes a place of constant contradiction between words and deeds, between the virtuous declarations or pretences of *all* the characters, and their actual actions: so that the play amounts to "a complicated examination of a corrupted society."[11]

In the introduction to her exemplary critical edition of *La bottega del caffè*, Roberta Turchi takes into account all these recent interpretations of the play, which in their extremism have the merit of suggesting that behind the apparent banality of the story lies a surprising wealth of themes.[12] Despite her use of these novel interpretations Turchi follows what remain, also in my opinion, the three best guides to the play: that of Eugenio Levi (1959), who anaylsed better than anybody else the character of Don Marzio ("blind hero" for his short-sightedness, and yet capable of detecting the contradictions and ambiguities of the characters surrounding him);[13] that of Mario Baratto (1962), who was the first to notice in the play "a kind of wide-spread infirmity";[14] and finally thatof Jacques Joly (1974), for whom the choice of the setting, an open *campiello* or small square in front of the coffee house, proceeds

> from the intention of opposing a choral, collective image
> of reality to the violence of passions, that is, from the intention of reminding us that each individual doesn't exist but
> in his relationship with all others, that the pursuit of happiness or the fulfillment of private passions shouldn't be at
> the expense of the community, of the harmonious organization of society.[15]

V.

If we go back to Goldoni's text armed with the readings I have cited, two things cannot fail to strike us. One is the sophisticated handling of the scenic space in relation to the action, to which Goldoni himself will call our attention in the foreword of his *Holiday Trilogy*

> . . . when the collective title encompasses a number of persons, unity is itself found in the multiplicity of the actions. To this genre belong (speaking of my own comedies) *Il teatro comico, La bottega del caffè* [. . .] All of the characters act toward the same end, and all of their different actions serve to advance the plot.[16]

On the one hand, *The Coffee House* is characterized by a horizontal space and movement, whereby from the small square minutely described at the beginning—a frontal block in the background with three establishments (a gambling house, coffee shop, and barber shop) topped by the gaming den, and in the wings, the inn on the left, the house of the dancer on the right—the intrigues and the effects of the gossip widen, like riples made by a stone entering water, to the city that ideally surrounds the stage. The two-way exchange between the invisible inner dwellings in the houses around the *campiello*, and the outer world beyond it, is stressed, as in a rhythmic scansion, by the frequent stage directions: *from the shop, from the inn, from the gambling house*; and conversely, *from the street*.

On the other hand, there is a vertical space and movement, whereby the worries and malignities generated, so to speak, at the ground level, in the barber shop or around Ridolfo's tables, rise to involve the characters who lean out of the windows upstairs, or whom we glimpse through those same windows. In the play's conclusion, all the victims of the finally unmasked slanderer address him from these upper windows, showering upon him the public reprobation that he so fully deserves.[17]

Another distinctive feature of the play is the triple series of oppositions running through it. Explicit oppositions and antitheses, first of all—between Pandolfo's dishonesty and Ridolfo's honesty; between the latter's reasonableness and Don Marzio's unreasonableness; between the professional conscience, again of the coffee house owner and the cynicism of his employee, Trappola; between the virtue of Vittoria and her husband's debauchery; between Eugenio's simplicity as a card player and the vicious skillfulness of Leandro; and so on and so forth. But also implicit oppositions, of which the author himself was perhaps only partially aware: between words and actions, as we have already seen (so that, for instance, the diplomas of virtue that the ballerina Lisaura and Eugenio so often grant to themselves are regularly belied by the facts); or between the commercial principles of Ridolfo and the expedients, more or less legitimate, that, as far as we know, were common practice among real coffee house owners—that is, if you want, between the edifying ends of the author, committed to his reform, and the "resistance" imposed upon these by Venetian reality.

Last but not least, contradictions and oppositions *within* the character of Don Marzio, make him a complex figure, different from Destouches' Damon or Gresset's Cléon:[18] short-sighted and voyeur, provided with a lorgnette that we may suppose powerful, and yet inclined to prefer what he imagines he is seeing or believes he has heard to what he does actually see or could see if he used his instrument better. Constantly on on the wrong track in his short-term surmising, that is, in his immediate reading of reality (on the time marked by his own watch, on the profession of the pilgrim, etc.), but a far more clear-sighted *moralist* as far as other *characters* are concerned (I am using the two words in their classical French meaning), as when he guesses Eugenio's erotic interest in the pilgrim, or when he hyperbolically voices the very suspicion that the self-proclaimed goodness of Eugenio, Vittoria, and Ridolfo rouses even in us, the spectators: "Here are the three fools. The mischievous fool, the jealous fool, and the glorious fool" (III, p. 163).

Thus, after all, many of our oppositions may well imply and

hide analogies or affinities. Eugenio's behavior toward his wife is no better than that of the cardsharp Leandro toward his; Ridolfo knows about his neighbors more than he is ready to admit (about the celebrated back door of the ballerina's house, for instance), and keeps silent out of convenience on what Don Marzio blurts out by irresponsability, and so on.

At this point, we may find more convincing a "double reading" of the comedy which its most subtle interpreters have suggested. To be sure, the square or *campiello*, with its practicable constructions and the various commercial activities integrated with the life of the city, illustrates and, in the end, recomposes that order, that virtuous sociability that Eugenio's profligacy, the frauds of Pandolfo and Leandro, the easy ways of the ballerina, but above all the slander of Don Marzio had threatened and temporarily used. In this sense Ridolfo—the former servant or *Zanni* promoted to property and bourgeois dignity—is indeed the hero of the play.

Still, a shadow hovers even about the "good" characters—a doubt remains in our mind about their motivations and their future. Then, Goldoni's *bottega*, which Ridolfo tried and in a way managed to redeem from the filthy uses that Narciso was making of it, is a far cry from those in the heart of London or Paris. A new culture was effectively taking shape: and this, in spite of all the acrobatic and erudite attempts of some recent critics.[19]

Rather than politics (a subject that was taboo in Venice) or philosophy, Ridolfo's patrons talk of the weather, with an admirable adherence to the trite discourse of every day:

> SERGEANT Fine weather we're having.
> DON MARZIO The weather won't last.
> SERGEANT Oh well. Let's enjoy it while it's good.
>
> (III, p. 155)

Or they talk of the troubles of a young merchant who neglects his wife and is gambling away his fortune; above all, they talk about money: in Act I a hundred sequins in cash lost by Eugenio, ten sequins he borrowed from Don Marzio, thirty sequins that Pandolfo offers to find him, with interest of a sequin a week (I, p. 21), thirty again paid to Eugenio by the honest Ridolfo as an advance on the sale of two bolts of cloth, and so on throughout the comedy.

This does not mean that Goldoni was not aware of other functions coffee houses could perform. Indeed this is ironically hinted at in "This English Philosopher." But our author knew only too well that Venice was not London or Paris (nor, we could add, Milan under Maria Theresa and von Kaunitz). Behind Ridolfo, we still perceive Brighella, and Eugenio, rather than a bourgeois, is a cortesan manqué.[20]

On the one hand, *The Coffee House* brings onto the stage a civilization in the existence of which Goldoni would like to believe without really succeeding: and this is the local, Venetian face of the play. On the other hand, Don Marzio—whose novelty as a character critics never missed—goes beyond this historical and geographic Venice.

The Neapolitan foreigner in Ridolfo's shop is not only a gossip, he is a radical pessimist who immediately finds the worst possible motivations for what people do. After their reunion, Leandro and Placida will tour the world swindling the fools out of their money ("Their whole income consists in a deck of cards"). And Eugenio has made peace with his wife because "he's ruined, and he hasn't anything left to live on. His wife is young and pretty. . . . He's thought this one out, and Ridolfo will be his go-between" (III, p. 167). Not only is Don Marzio inordinately proud of his nobility, never missing an opportunity of spiteing and abusing the commoners he deals with; he is also literally possessed by the spirit of contradiction, so that, when someone else repeats verbatim one of his own statements, that statement becomes immediately untrue, like his dialogue with Leandro, first about military matters and then about snuff (II, pp. 111-115), in which the possibility of reaching a reasonable conclusion on anything whatever fades hopelessly away. Finally, Don Marzio cannot be alone, he must fill the void of his life by talking to somebody behind everybody's back, out of the same need of—and aversion to—the others, which gives no rest to Poe's mysterious and sinister *man of the crowd*. Poe's character, we remember, "who refuses to be alone," and, adds the author, is like a book that does not permit itself to be read.

Between the farcical or reckless situations inherited from the Commedia dell'Arte and the moral program trusted to the sermonizing Ridolfo; between the ideal coffee houses of the Enlightenment and the culturally modest shops of Venice, our comedy seems to remain half way. However—and here we see Goldoni's mastery as a playwright—the dissatisfaction or malaise that such a tension could cause is embodied and finally resolved in a figure at the same time credible and elusive, that of the slanderer. Through his activity, the theatrical discourse exerts on reality, in an oblique manner, a cognitive or diagnostic power, to which in Venice, the culture of the books and of the schools could not aspire for the moment.

LA BOTTEGA DEL CAFFÈ

THE COFFEE HOUSE

Commedia di tre atti in prosa.
Rappresentata per la prima volta in Mantova
la Primavera dell'Anno MDCCL

Prose comedy in three acts
Performed for the first time in Mantua
in the Spring of 1750

L'AUTORE A CHI LEGGE

Quando composi da prima la presente commedia, lo feci col Brighella e coll'Arlecchino, ed ebbe, a dir vero, felicissimo incontro, per ogni parte. Ciò non ostante dandola io alle stampe, ho creduto meglio servire il pubblico, rendendola più universale, cambiando in essa non solamente in toscano i due personaggi suddetti, ma tre altri ancora, che col dialetto veneziano parlavano.

Corse in Firenze una commedia con simil titolo e con vari accidenti a questa simili, perché da questa copiati. Un amico mio di talento e di spirito fece prova di sua memoria; ma avendola una, o due volte sole veduta rappresentare in Milano, molte cose da lui inventate dovette per necessità framischiarvi. Donata ho all'amicizia la burla, ed ho lodato l'ingegno; nulladimeno, né voglio arrogarmi il buono, che non è mio, né voglio che passi per mia qualche cosa, che mi dispiace.

Ho voluto pertanto informare il pubblico di un simil fatto, perché confrontandosi la mia, che ora io stampo, con quella dell'amico suddetto, sia palese la verità, e ciascheduno profitti della sua porzione di lode, e della sua porzione di biasimo si contenti.

Questa commedia ha caratteri tanto universali, che in ogni luogo ove fu ella rappresentata, credevasi fatta sul conio degli originali riconosciuti. Il Maldicente fra gli altri trovò il suo prototipo da per tutto, e mi convenne soffrir talora, benché innocente, la taccia d'averlo maliziosamente copiato. No certamente, non son capace di farlo.

I miei caratteri sono umani, sono verisimili, e forse veri, ma io gli traggo dalla turba universale degli uomini, e vuole il caso che alcuno in essi si riconosca. Quando ciò accade, non è mia colpa che il carattere tristo a quel vizioso somigli; ma colpa è del vizioso, che dal carattere ch'io dipingo, trovasi per sua sventura attaccato.

THE AUTHOR TO THE READER

When I first wrote the present comedy, I used the characters Brighella and Arlecchino and, to tell the truth, it enjoyed success everywhere. In spite of this, in giving it to the press, I believed that I could better serve the public by rendering it more universal. I thus changed to Tuscan not only the language of the two characters mentioned above, but also that of three others who spoke in the Venetian dialect.

Another comedy ran in Florence with a similar title and various incidents which, having been copied from my comedy, made it similar to mine. A talented and witty friend of mine put his memory to the test: but having seen my comedy performed in Milan only once or twice, he inevitably mixed in many things of his own invention. I have attributed the prank to friendship and praised its ingenuity. Nonetheless, I do not want to take credit for the worthy parts which are not mine, nor do I want something I find distasteful to pass for something of mine.

I wish, therefore, to inform the public of the matter so that when my comedy—which I am now publishing—is compared with that of my above mentioned friend, the truth may be evident and each of us profit from his portion of praise and content himself with his portion of criticism.

The characters of this comedy are so familiar that wherever it has been performed, they have been thought to be drawn from recognizable originals. The Scandalmonger, in particular, found his prototype everywhere, and, despite my innocence, I have at times been forced to suffer the accusation of having maliciously copied it—something I am certainly not capable of doing.

My characters are human, lifelike, and maybe even real. The fact is that I draw them from the universal throng of men, and it so happens that some people recognize themselves in them. When this occurs, it is not my fault that the wretched character resembles a certain depraved person. It is that depraved person's fault that, to his misfortune, he finds himself lambasted by the character that I portray.

Personaggi

RIDOLFO, *caffettiere.*
DON MARZIO, *gentiluomo napolitano.*
EUGENIO, *mercante.*
FLAMMINIO, *sotto nome di conte Leandro.*
PLACIDA, *moglie di Flamminio, in abito di pellegrina.*
VITTORIA, *moglie di Eugenio.*
LISAURA, *ballerina.*
PANDOLFO, *biscazziere.*
TRAPPOLA, *garzone di Ridolfo.*
UN GARZONE *del parrucchiere, che parla.*
ALTRO GARZONE *del caffettiere, che parla.*
UN CAMERIERE *di locanda, che parla.*
CAPITANO *di birri, che parla.*
Birri, *che non parlano.*
Altri Camerieri *di locanda, che non parlano.*
Altri Garzoni *della bottega di caffè, che non parlano.*

La scena stabile rappresenta una piazzetta in Venezia, ovvero una strada alquanto spaziosa con tre botteghe: quella di mezzo ad uso di caffè, quella alla diritta di parrucchiere e barbiere, quella alla sinistra ad uso di giuoco, o sia biscazza; e sopra le tre botteghe suddette si vedono alcuni stanzini praticabili appartenenti alla bisca colle finestre in veduta della strada medesima. Dalla parte del barbiere (con una strada in mezzo) evvi la casa della ballerina, e dalla parte della bisca vedesi la locanda, con porte e finestre praticabili.

Characters

RIDOLFO, *owner of the coffee house*
DON MARZIO, *Neopolitan gentleman*
EUGENIO, *merchant*
FLAMINIO, *under the name of Count Leandro*
PLACIDA, *Flaminio's wife, dressed as a wayfarer*
VITTORIA, *Eugenio's wife*
LISAURA, *dancer*
PANDOLFO, *Owner of the gambling house*
TRAPPOLA, *Ridolfo's Boy*
A BOY *from the Wig-maker, who speaks*
ANOTHER BOY *from the coffee house, who speaks*
A WAITER *from the Inn, who speaks*
A POLICE SERGEANT *with his men, who speaks*
Other Policemen *who do not speak*
Other Waiters *from the Inn, who do not speak*
Other Boys *from the coffee house, who do not speak*

The permanent scene is a small square in Venice, or an equally spacious street, with three shops: the one in the middle used as a cafe, the one on the right as a wig-maker and barbershop, the one of the left used as a gambling house or card room. Above the shops some accessible rooms, which belong to the gambling house, its windows overlooking the street. The dancer's house is on the side of the barbershop (with a street in between), and the inn, with functioning doors and windows, is on the side of the gambling house.

ATTO PRIMO

SCENA I

RIDOLFO, TRAPPOLA *e altri garzoni*

RIDOLFO Animo, figliuoli, portatevi bene; siate lesti e pronti a
servir gli avventori, con civiltà, con proprietà: perché tante
volte dipende il credito di una bottega, dalla buona
maniera di quei che servono.

TRAPPOLA Caro signor padrone, per dirvi la verità: questo
levarsi di buon'ora non è niente fatto per la mia
complessione.

RIDOLFO Eppure bisogna levarsi presto. Bisogna servir tutti. A
buon'ora vengono quelli che hanno da far viaggio, i
lavoranti, i barcaruoli, i marinai, tutta gente, che si alza di
buon mattino.

TRAPPOLA È veramente una cosa che fa crepar di ridere, veder
anche i facchini venir a bevere il loro caffè.

RIDOLFO Tutti cercan di fare quello che fanno gli altri. Una
volta correva l'acquavite, adesso è in voga il caffè.

TRAPPOLA E quella signora, dove porto il caffè tutte le mattine,
quasi sempre mi prega che io le compri quattro soldi di
legna, e pur vuol bevere il suo caffè.

RIDOLFO La gola è un vizio, che non finisce mai, ed è quel
vizio, che cresce sempre quanto più l'uomo invecchia.

TRAPPOLA Non si vede venir nessuno a bottega; si poteva
dormire un'altra oretta.

RIDOLFO Or ora verrà della gente; non è poi tanto di buon'ora.
Non vedete? Il barbiere ha aperto, è in bottega lavorando
parrucche. Guarda, anche il botteghino del giuoco è aperto.

TRAPPOLA Oh in quanto poi a questa biscazza è aperta che è un
pezzo. Hanno fatto nottata.

ACT ONE

SCENE I

RIDOLFO, TRAPPOLA *and other boys*

RIDOLFO Come on, lads. Be good. Be quick and ready
to serve our customers politely, with civility. Because the
reputation of a shop often rests on the good manners of
its servants.

TRAPPOLA My dear master, to tell the truth, this early rising
isn't any good for my constitution.

RIDOLFO Nonetheless, we have to get up early. We have
to serve everyone. At this hour travelers, workmen,
boatmen, and sailors come, all the people who rise
with the dawn.

TRAPPOLA It's really enough to make one die laughing, to see
even the porters come to have their coffee.

RIDOLFO Everybody tries to do what everyone else does. There
was a time when brandy was the rage; now it's coffee.

TRAPPOLA And that lady, where I bring the coffee every morning, she almost always asks me to buy her a measly four-
farthing's worth of firewood. Yet even she wants to have
her coffee.

RIDOLFO Gluttony is a never-ending vice, and it grows
with age.

TRAPPOLA I don't see anyone coming to our shop. We could
have slept for another hour.

RIDOLFO People will come soon enough. It's not so early.
Don't you see? The barber's open. He's in his shop working
on his wigs. Look, the gambling house is open too.

TRAPPOLA Oh, that card room's been open for a while. They
made a night of it.

RIDOLFO Buono. A messer Pandolfo avrà fruttato bene.

TRAPPOLA A quel cane frutta sempre bene; guadagna
nelle carte, guadagna negli scrocchi, guadagna a far
di balla coi barattieri. I denari di chi va là dentro,
sono tutti suoi.

RIDOLFO Non v'innamoraste mai di questo guadagno, perché
la farina del diavolo va tutta in crusca.

TRAPPOLA Quel povero signore Eugenio! Lo ha precipitato.

IRIDOLFO Guardate anche quegli, che poco giudizio! Ha
moglie, una giovane di garbo e di proposito, e corre
dietro a tutte le donne, e poi di più giuoca da
disperato.

TRAPPOLA Piccole galanterie della gioventù moderna.

RIDOLFO Giuoca con quel conte Leandro, e gli ha persi
sicuri.

TRAPPOLA Oh quel signor conte è un bel fior di virtù.

RIDOLFO Oh via, andate a tostare il caffè, per farne una
caffettiera di fresco.

TRAPPOLa Vi metto degli avanzi di ieri sera?

RIDOLFO No, fatelo buono.

TRAPPOLA Signor padrone, ho poca memoria. Quant'è che
avete aperto bottega?

RIDOLFO Lo sapete pure. Saranno in circa otto mesi.

TRAPPOLA È tempo da mutar costume.

RIDOLFO Come sarebbe a dire?

TRAPPOLA Quando si apre una bottega nuova, si fa il caffè
perfetto. Dopo sei mesi al più, acqua calda e brodo lungo.
(*parte*)

RIDOLFO È grazioso costui. Spero che farà bene per la
mia bottega; perché in quelle botteghe, dove vi è
qualcheduno, che sappia fare il buffone, tutti corrono.

RIDOLFO Well, then. Things must be good for Master Pandolfo.

TRAPPOLA Things are always good for that dog. He profits in cards, he profits in sponging, he profits in the understandings he has with the cardsharps. Every penny that goes in there is his.

RIDOLFO Don't ever fall in love with such profit, for you know that the devil's meal is half bran.

TRAPPOLA And poor Signor Eugenio's been ruined.

RIDOLFO There's a fool for you. He doesn't have any sense! He's married to a charming and sensible young lady, yet he runs after every woman in sight. And besides that, he gambles like a madman.

TRAPPOLA Gallantries of modern youth!

RIDOLFO He's playing with that Count Leandro, and he's lost his money for sure.

TRAPPOLA Oh, that Count Leandro is a rare flower of virtue!

RIDOLFO Well, run along. Go roast the coffee, and make a fresh pot.

TRAPPOLA Shall I use yesterday's leftovers?

RIDOLFO No. Make it fresh.

TRAPPOLA Dear master, I have a poor memory. How long have you been open here?

RIDOLFO You know perfectly well. About eight months.

TRAPPOLA Then it's time to change our ways.

RIDOLFO What is that supposed to mean?

TRAPPOLA When you first open a shop, you make perfect coffee. But after six months—at the most—lots of hot water and the soup lasts longer! (exit Trappola)

RIDOLFO Witty, that fellow. I hope he'll be good for business. For wherever there's someone to play the fool, the crowd will gather.

ie. Trappola — actually does "boy" here, just mean servant-he seems old

SCENA II

RIDOLFO, *e messer* PANDOLFO *dalla bottega del giuoco trofinandosi gl'occhi come assonnato*

RIDOLFO Messer Pandolfo, volete il caffè?

PANDOLFO Sì, mi farete piacere.

RIDOLFO Giovani, date il caffè a messer Pandolfo. Sedete, accomodatevi.

PANDOLFO No, no, bisogna che io lo beva presto, e che ritorni al travaglio. (*un giovane porta il caffè a Pandolfo*)

RIDOLFO Giuocano ancora in bottega?

PANDOLFO Si lavora a due telai.

RIDOLFO Così presto?

PANDOLFO Giuocano da ieri in qua.

RIDOLFO A che giuoco?

PANDOLFO A un giuoco innocente: *prima, e seconda.*

RIDOLFO E come va?

PANDOLFO Per me va bene.

RIDOLFO Vi siete divertito anche voi a giuocare?

PANDOLFO Sì, anch'io ho tagliato un poco.

RIDOLFO Compatite, amico, io non ho da entrare ne' vostri interessi; ma non istà bene che il padrone della bottega giuochi, perché se perde, si fa burlare, e se guadagna, fa sospettare.

PANDOLFO A me basta che non mi burlino; del resto poi, che sospettino quanto vogliono, non ci penso.

RIDOLFO Caro amico, siamo vicini, e non vorrei che vi accadessero delle disgrazie. Sapete che per il vostro giuoco siete stato dell'altre volte in cattura.

PANDOLFO Mi contento di poco. Ho buscati due zecchini, e non ho voluto altro.

RIDOLFO Bravo, pelar la quaglia senza farla gridare. A chi gli avete vinti?

PANDOLFO Ad un garzone d'un orefice.

RIDOLFO Male, malissimo; così si dà mano ai giovani, perché rubino ai loro padroni.

SCENE II

Enter master PANDOLFO *from his gambling house, rubbing his eyes as if sleepy*

RIDOLFO Master Pandolfo, would you like a coffee?

PANDOLFO If you would be so obliging.

RIDOLFO Boys, give Master Pandolfo his coffee. Sit down. Make yourself comfortable.

PANDOLFO No, no. I have to drink it in a hurry and get back to my work. (*a boy brings Pandolfo his coffee*)

RIDOLFO Are they still playing at your place?

PANDOLFO Two looms are working.

RIDOLFO This early?

PANDOLFO They've been playing since yesterday.

RIDOLFO What are they playing?

PANDOLFO An innocent little game of faro.

RIDOLFO And how are things going?

PANDOLFO Well enough, for me.

RIDOLFO Have you been playing too?

PANDOLFO Yes, I cut the cards a few times as well.

RIDOLFO Bear with me, my friend—it's not my place to meddle in your affairs—but it doesn't look good when the owner of the house plays as well, because if he loses, he's laughed at, and if he wins he's suspect.

PANDOLFO As long as they don't make fun of me. Anyhow, let them suspect as much as they want. It doesn't bother me.

RIDOLFO My dear friend, you and I are neighbors, and I wouldn't want anything bad to happen to you. You know that you've been arrested more than once for this gambling of yours.

PANDOLFO I'm not greedy. I pocketed two sequins, and that was enough for me.

RIDOLFO Good man. You pluck the fowl without making it squawk. Who'd you win them from?

PANDOLFO A goldsmith's apprentice.

RIDOLFO Bad, bad indeed. That's how boys are inspired to steal from their masters.

PANDOLFO Eh non mi venite a moralizzare. Chi è gonzo stia a
casa sua. Io tengo giuoco per chi vuol giuocare.

RIDOLFO Tener giuoco stimo il meno; ma voi siete preso
di mira per giuocator di vantaggio, e in questa sorta di
cose si fa presto a precipitare.

PANDOLFO Io bricconate non ne fo. So giuocare; son fortunato,
e per questo vinco.

RIDOLFO Bravo, tirate innanzi così. Il signor Eugenio ha
giuocato questa notte?

PANDOLFO Giuoca anche adesso. Non ha cenato, non ha
dormito, e ha perso tutti i denari.

RIDOLFO (Povero giovine!) Quanto averà perduto?

PANDOLFO Cento zecchini in contanti; e ora perde sulla
parola.

RIDOLFO Con chi giuoca?

PANDOLFO Col signor conte.

RIDOLFO Con quello sì fatto?

PANDOLFO Appunto con quello.

RIDOLFO E con chi altri?

PANDOLFO Essi due soli: a testa a testa.

RIDOLFO Poveraccio! Sta fresco davvero.

PANDOLFO Che importa? A me basta che scozzino delle carte
assai.

RIDOLFO Non terrei giuoco, se credessi di farmi ricco.

PANDOLFO No? Per qual ragione?

RIDOLFO Mi pare che un galantuomo non debba soffrire di
vedere assassinar la gente.

PANDOLFO Eh, amico, se sarete così delicato di pelle, farete
pochi quattrini.

RIDOLFO Non me ne importa niente. Fin'ora sono stato a
servire, e ho fatto il mio debito onoratamente. Mi
sono avanzato quattro soldi, e coll'aiuto del mio
padrone d'allora, ch'era il padre, come sapete, del
signor Eugenio, ho aperta questa bottega, e con
questa voglio vivere onoratamente, e non voglio far
torto alla mia professione.

PANDOLFO Oh, spare me your morals. Let the dunces stay at home. I'll keep play for whoever wants to gamble.

RIDOLFO Running card games is bad enough, but you'll be marked as someone who's not above cheating, and in that sort of thing, one is quick to fall.

PANDOLFO I play no tricks. I know how to play. I'm lucky, and so I win.

RIDOLFO Very well, do things your way. Did Signor Eugenio play last night?

PANDOLFO In fact, he's still playing. He had no supper, nor did he sleep. And he's lost all his money.

RIDOLFO (aside) Poor fellow! (to Pandolfo) How much could he have lost?

PANDOLFO A hundred sequins in cash. And now he's losing on his word.

RIDOLFO Who's he playing with?

PANDOLFO With the Count.

RIDOLFO With someone like that?

PANDOLFO With him, precisely.

RIDOLFO And with who else?

PANDOLFO Just those two, head to head.

RIDOLFO Poor devil! He's really in for it!

PANDOLFO So what! As long as they keep on shuffling the cards.

RIDOLFO I wouldn't run such games, even if I believed it would make me rich.

PANDOLFO No? Why not?

RIDOLFO It seems to me that a gentleman couldn't just stand by, watching people be killed.

PANDOLFO Well, my friend, if you are as soft-hearted as that, you'll never make much money.

RIDOLFO I couldn't care less. Up to now, I've been a servant and fulfilled my task with honor. I saved a few pennies, and with some help from my former master—who, as you know, was Signor Eugenio's father—I opened this shop and I want to make an honorable living with it, without discrediting my profession.

PANDOLFO Oh anche nella vostra professione vi sono de' bei capi d'opera!

RIDOLFO Ve ne sono in tutte le professioni. Ma da quelli non vanno le persone ragguardevoli, che vengono alla mia bottega.

PANDOLFO Avete anche voi gli stanzini segreti.

RIDOLFO È vero; ma non si chiude la porta.

PANDOLFO Il caffè, non potete negarlo a nessuno.

RIDOLFO Le chicchere non si macchiano.

PANDOLFO Eh via! Si serra un occhio.

RIDOLFO Non si serra niente; in questa bottega non vien che gente onorata.

PANDOLFO Sì, sì, siete principiante.

RIDOLFO Che vorreste dire? (*gente dalla bottega del giuoco chiama:* carte)

PANDOLFO La servo. (*verso la sua bottega*)

RIDOLFO Per carità, levate dal tavolino quel povero signor Eugenio.

PANDOLFO Per me, che perda anche la camicia, non ci penso. (*s'incammina verso la sua bottega*)

RIDOLFO Amico, il caffè ho da notarlo?

PANDOLFO Niente, lo giuocheremo a primiera.

RIDOLFO Io non son gonzo, amico.

PANDOLFO Via, che serve? Sapete pure che i miei avventori si servono alla vostra bottega. Mi maraviglio che attendiate a queste piccole cose. (*s'incammina*)
(*Tornano a chiamare*)

PANDOLFO Eccomi. (*entra nel giuoco*)

RIDOLFO Bel mestiere! Vivere sulle disgrazie, sulla rovina della gioventù! Per me, non vi sarà mai pericolo che tenga giuoco. Si principia con i giuochetti, e poi si termina colla bassetta. No, no, caffè, caffè; giacché col caffè si guadagna il cinquanta per cento, che cosa vogliamo cercar di più?

PANDOLFO Well, even in your profession there are some true gems.

RIDOLFO There are in all professions. But the distinguished people who come to my shop don't mix with them.

PANDOLFO You too have your private rooms.

RIDOLFO True. But I don't shut the doors.

PANDOLFO You can't refuse coffee to anyone.

RIDOLFO Coffee-cups aren't market.

PANDOLFO Oh, come! You look the other way.

RIDOLFO I do no such thing. In this shop you'll find only respectable people.

PANDOLFO Yes, yes. You're still green.

RIDOLFO What's that supposed to mean? (*people call from the gambling house:*) Cards!

PANDOLFO (*toward his gambling house*) Right away.

RIDOLFO For Heaven's sake, get poor Eugenio away from that table!

PANDOLFO He can lose the shirt off his back for all I care. (*starts to walk toward his gambling house*)

RIDOLFO My friend, the coffee? Shall I put it on your bill?

PANDOLFO No. We'll play for it at primero.

RIDOLFO I'm no dunce, friend.

PANDOLFO Why talk like that? You know full well that my customers come to your shop too. I'm surprised that you bother with such trifles. (*starts to walk*)
(*more calls from the gambling house*)

PANDOLFO Here I am. (*enters the gambling house*)

RIDOLFO A fine profession! To live on the misfortunes and ruination of youth. As for me, there's no chance that I'll ever allow gambling. One begins with party-games and ends with basset. No, no, coffee, coffee. It brings in fifty per cent. What more can we ask?

SCENA III

DON MARZIO *e* RIDOLFO

RIDOLFO (Ecco qui quel che non tace mai, e che sempre vuole aver ragione). (*da sé*)

DON MARZIO Caffè.

RIDOLFO Subito, sarà servita.

DON MARZIO Che vi è di nuovo, Ridolfo?

RIDOLFO Non saprei, signore.

DON MARZIO Non si è ancora veduto nessuno a questa vostra bottega?

RIDOLFO È per anco buon'ora.

DON MARZIO Buon'ora? Sono sedeci ore sonate.

RIDOLFO Oh illustrissimo no, non sono ancora quattordici.

DON MARZIO Eh via, buffone.

RIDOLFO Le assicuro io, che le quattordici non son sonate.

DON MARZIO Eh via, asino.

RIDOLFO Ella mi strapazza senza ragione.

DON MARZIO Ho contato in questo punto le ore, e vi dico, che sono sedici; e poi guardate il mio orologio: questo non fallisce mai. (*gli mostra l'orologio*)

RIDOLFO Bene; se il suo orologio non fallisce, osservi: il suo orologio medesimo mostra tredici ore e tre quarti.

DON MARZIO Eh, non può essere. (*cava l'occhialetto e guarda*)

RIDOLFO Che dice?

DON MARZIO Il mio orologio va male. Sono sedici ore. Le ho sentite io.

RIDOLFO Dove l'ha comprato quell'orologio?

DON MARZIO L'ho fatto venir di Londra.

RIDOLFO L'hanno ingannata.

DON MARZIO Mi hanno ingannato? Perché?

RIDOLFO Le hanno mandato un orologio cattivo. (*ironicamente*)

DON MARZIO Come cattivo? È uno dei più perfetti che abbia fatto il Quarè.

RIDOLFO Se fosse buono, non fallirebbe di due ore.

DON MARZIO Questo va sempre bene, non fallisce mai.

SCENE III

Enter DON MARZIO

RIDOLFO (*aside*) Here's the one who never shuts up, and insists on being right all the time.

DON MARZIO Coffee.

RIDOLFO Right away, at your service.

DON MARZIO What's new, Ridolfo?

RIDOLFO I wouldn't know, sir.

DON MARZIO Haven't you seen anyone yet in this shop of yours?

RIDOLFO It's still very early.

DON MARZIO Early? It's well past nine.

RIDOLFO Oh no, your grace, it's not yet seven o'clock.

DON MARZIO Oh come, joker.

RIDOLFO I assure you that it hasn't yet struck seven.

DON MARZIO Oh come, you ass.

RIDOLFO You're getting rough with me for no reason.

DON MARZIO I've counted the bells to this point, and I'm telling you that it's nine o'clock. And anyway, look at my watch: it's never wrong. (*shows him the watch*)

RIDOLFO Well, if your watch is never wrong, look at this: your own watch reads six and three quarters.

DON MARZIO Oh, that can't be. (*takes out his lorgnette and looks*)

RIDOLFO What does it say?

DON MARZIO My watch isn't right. It's nine o'clock. I heard the tolls myself.

RIDOLFO Where did you buy that watch?

DON MARZIO I sent for it from London.

RIDOLFO They swindled you.

DON MARZIO They swindled me? Why do you say that?

RIDOLFO (*ironically*) They sent you a bad watch.

DON MARZIO What do you mean, bad? It's one of the most perfect Quares ever made.

RIDOLFO If it were good, it wouldn't be off by two hours.

DON MARZIO This watch always runs well. It's never wrong.

RIDOLFO Ma se fa quattordici ore meno un quarto, e dice che sono sedici.

DON MARZIO Il mio orologio va bene.

RIDOLFO Dunque saranno or ora quattordici, come dico io.

DON MARZIO Sei un temerario. Il mio orologio va bene, tu di' male, e guarda ch'io non ti dia qualche cosa nel capo. (*un giovane porta il caffè*)

RIDOLFO È servita del caffè. (*con isdegno*) (Oh che bestiaccia!) (*da sé*)

DON MARZIO Si è veduto il signor Eugenio?

RIDOLFO Illustrissimo signor no.

DON MARZIO Sarà in casa a carezzare la moglie. Che uomo effemminato! Sempre moglie! Sempre moglie! Non si lascia più vedere; si fa ridicolo. È un uomo di stucco. Non sa quel che si faccia. Sempre moglie, sempre moglie. (*bevendo il caffè*)

RIDOLFO Altro che moglie! È stato tutta la notte a giuocare qui da messer Pandolfo.

DON MARZIO Se lo dico io. Sempre giuoco! Sempre giuoco! (*dà la chicchera, e s'alza*)

RIDOLFO (Sempre giuoco; sempre moglie; sempre il diavolo, che se lo porti). (*da sé*)

DON MARZIO È venuto da me l'altro giorno con tutta segretezza a pregarmi che gli prestassi dieci zecchini sopra un paio d'orecchini di sua moglie.

RIDOLFO Vede bene; tutti gli uomini sono soggetti ad avere qualche volta bisogno; ma non hanno piacere poi che si sappia, e per questo sarà venuto da lei, sicuro che non dirà niente a nessuno.

DON MARZIO Oh io non parlo. Fo volentieri servizio a tutti, e non me ne vanto. Eccoli qui; questi sono gli orecchini di sua moglie. Gli ho prestato dieci zecchini; vi pare che io sia al coperto? (*mostra gli orecchini in una custodia*)

RIDOLFO Io non me ne intendo, ma mi par di sì.

DON MARZIO Avete il vostro garzone?

RIDOLFO Vi sarà.

DON MARZIO Chiamatelo. Ehi Trappola.

RIDOLFO But if it reads a quarter till seven, and you say that it's nine.

DON MARZIO My watch runs fine.

RIDOLFO Then it's just about seven, as I was saying.

DON MARZIO You fool. My watch runs fine. Watch your tongue or I'll smack you on the head. (*a boy brings his coffee*)

RIDOLFO (*with disdain*) Here's your coffee, sir. (*aside*) Oh, what a blockhead.

DON MARZIO Have you seen Signor Eugenio?

RIDOLFO No, your grace.

DON MARZIO (*drinking his coffee*) He's probably at home petting his wife. What an effeminate man! Always his wife! It's always his wife! He doesn't show himself around here anymore. He's becoming ridiculous. What a bore. He doesn't know what he's doing. Always his wife, always his wife.

RIDOLFO It's everything but his wife! He was here all night playing cards at Master Pandolfo's.

DON MARZIO As I was saying. It's always gambling! Always gambling! (*gives Ridolfo the cup, and stands*)

RIDOLFO (*aside*) It's always gambling. It's always his wife. It's always the devil: the devil take him.

DON MARZIO He came to me the other day, in great secrecy, begging me to lend him ten sequins on a pair of his wife's earrings.

RIDOLFO You see, all men may find themselves in need, but for this need to be known, none of them like it. That's probably why he came to you, sure that you wouldn't say anything to anyone.

DON MARZIO Oh, I don't gossip. I'm happy to be of service to everyone, and I don't brag about it. Here they are. These are his wife's earrings. I lent him ten sequins. Do you think I'm covered? (*shows him the earrings in a case*)

RIDOLFO I'm no expert, but it seems so.

DON MARZIO Do you have your boy here?

RIDOLFO He should be here.

DON MARZIO Call him. Hey, Trappola.

SCENA IV

TRAPPOLA *dall'interno della bottega, e detti*

TRAPPOLA Eccomi.

DON MARZIO Vieni qui. Va' dal gioielliere qui vicino, fagli
vedere questi orecchini, che sono della moglie del signor
Eugenio, e dimandagli da parte mia, se io sono al coperto
di dieci zecchini, che gli ho prestati.

TRAPPOLA Sarà servita. Dunque questi orecchini sono della
moglie del signor Eugenio?

DON MARZIO Sì, or ora non ha più niente; è morto di fame.

RIDOLFO (Meschino, in che mani è capitato!) (*da sé*)

TRAPPOLA E al signor Eugenio non importa niente di far sapere
i fatti suoi a tutti?

DON MARZIO Io sono una persona, alla quale si può confidare
un segreto.

TRAPPOLA Ed io sono una persona, alla quale non si può
confidar niente.

DON MARZIO Perché?

TRAPPOLA Perché ho un vizio, che ridico tutto con facilità.

DON MARZIO Male, malissimo; se farai così, perderai il credito,
e nessuno si fiderà di te.

TRAPPOLA Ma come ella l'ha detto a me, così io posso dirlo ad
un altro.

DON MARZIO Va a vedere, se il barbiere è a tempo per farmi la
barba.

TRAPPOLA La servo. (Per dieci quattrini vuol bevere il caffè, e
vuole un servitore al suo comando). (*entra dal barbiere*)

DON MARZIO Ditemi Ridolfo: che cosa fa quella ballerina qui
vicina?

RIDOLFO In verità, non so niente.

DON MARZIO Mi è stato detto che il conte Leandro la tiene
sotto la sua tutela.

RIDOLFO Con grazia, signore, il caffè vuol bollire. (Voglio
badare a' fatti miei). (*entra in bottega*)

SCENE IV

Enter TRAPPOLA *from the back of the shop*

TRAPPOLA Here I am.

DON MARZIO Come here. Go to the jeweler nearby. Show him these earrings that belong to Signor Eugenio's wife, and ask him, on my behalf, if I'm covered for the ten sequins that I lent him.

TRAPPOLA At your service, sir. Let's see. These earrings belong to Signor Eugenio's wife?

DON MARZIO Yes, in a little while he won't have anything left. He's down on his uppers.

RIDOLFO (*aside*) Poor fellow, what hands he's fallen into!

TRAPPOLA And doesn't Signor Eugenio mind making his affairs known to all?

DON MARZIO I'm someone you can trust with a secret.

TRAPPOLA And I'm someone not to be trusted at all.

DON MARZIO Why?

TRAPPOLA Because I have a vice: I repeat everything freely.

DON MARZIO Bad, bad indeed. If you act like that, you will lose credit, and no one will trust you.

TRAPPOLA But just as you told it to me, likewise I can tell it to someone else.

DON MARZIO Go see if the barber is ready to give me a shave.

TRAPPOLA Right away, sir. (*aside*) For ten farthings he wants to have his coffee, and he wants a servant at his command. (*enters the barbershop*)

DON MARZIO Tell me, Ridolfo, what does she do, that dancer who lives around here?

RIDOLFO To be honest, I don't know anything about her.

DON MARZIO I've been told that Count Leandro keeps her under his tutelage.

RIDOLFO Please excuse me, sir, the coffee is about to boil. (*aside*) I mind my own business. (*enters the shop*)

SCENA V

TRAPPOLA *e* DON MARZIO

TRAPPOLA Il barbiere ha uno sotto; subito che averà finito di scorticar quello, servirà V.S. illustrissima.

DON MARZIO Dimmi: sai niente tu di quella ballerina, che sta qui vicino?

TRAPPOLA Della signora Lisaura?

DON MARZIO Sì.

TRAPPOLA So, e non so.

DON MARZIO Raccontami qualche cosa.

TRAPPOLA Se racconterò i fatti degli altri, perderò il credito, e nessuno si fiderà più di me.

DON MARZIO A me lo puoi dire. Sai chi sono, io non parlo. Il conte Leandro la pratica?

TRAPPOLA Alle sue ore la pratica.

DON MARZIO Che vuol dire alle sue ore?

TRAPPOLA Vuol dire, quando non è in caso di dar soggezione.

DON MARZIO Bravo; ora capisco. È un amico di buon cuore, che non vuole recarle pregiudizio.

TRAPPOLA Anzi desidera che la si profitti, per far partecipe anche lui delle sue care grazie.

DON MARZIO Meglio! Oh che Trappola malizioso! Va' via, va' a far vedere gli orecchini.

TRAPPOLA Al gioielliere lo posso dire, che sono della moglie del signor Eugenio?

DON MARZIO Sì, diglielo pure.

TRAPPOLA (Fra il signor Don Marzio ed io, formiamo una bellissima segretaria).

(*parte*)

SCENE V

Enter TRAPPOLA

TRAPPOLA The barber has someone in his chair. As soon as he's finished skinning him, he'll be with your grace.

DON MARZIO Say, do you know anything about that dancer who lives around here?

TRAPPOLA Signora Lisaura?

DON MARZIO Yes.

TRAPPOLA I do, and I don't.

DON MARZIO Tell me something.

TRAPPOLA If I tell about other people's affairs, I'll lose my credit, and no one will trust me anymore.

DON MARZIO You can tell me. You know me. I don't gossip. Does Count Leandro call on her?

TRAPPOLA When it's convenient, he calls on her.

DON MARZIO What does convenient mean?

TRAPPOLA It means when it doesn't create embarrassment.

DON MARZIO Good man. Now I understand. He's a dear friend of hers, and he doesn't want to wrong her.

TRAPPOLA Just the opposite: he wishes her to do well so that he too can share in her precious charms.

DON MARZIO Better yet! Oh, aren't you malicious, Trappola! Off with you, go and have the earrings looked at.

TRAPPOLA May I tell the jeweler that they belong to Signor Eugenio's wife?

DON MARZIO Yes, go ahead and tell him.

TRAPPOLA *(aside)* Don Marzio and myself, what a fine pair of confidants we make.
(exit Trappola)

SCENA VI

DON MARZIO, *poi* RIDOLFO

DON MARZIO Ridolfo.

RIDOLFO Signore.

DON MARZIO Se voi non sapete niente della ballerina, vi racconterò io.

RIDOLFO Io per dirgliela, dei fatti degli altri, non me ne curo molto.

DON MARZIO Ma sta bene saper qualche cosa per potersi regolare. Ella è protetta da quella buona pezza del conte Leandro, ed egli dai profitti della ballerina ricava il prezzo della sua protezione. In vece di spendere, mangia tutto a quella povera diavola; e per cagione di lui forse è costretta a fare quello che non farebbe. Oh che briccone!

RIDOLFO Ma io son qui tutto il giorno, e posso attestare che in casa sua non vedo andare altri che il conte Leandro.

DON MARZIO Ha la porta di dietro; pazzo, pazzo. Sempre, flusso, e riflusso. Ha la porta di dietro, pazzo.

RIDOLFO Io bado alla mia bottega, s'ella ha la porta di dietro che importa a me? Io non vado a dar di naso a nessuno.

DON MARZIO Bestia! Così parli con un par mio? (*s'alza*)

RIDOLFO Le domando perdono, non si può dire una facezia?

DON MARZIO Dammi un bicchier di rosolio.

RIDOLFO (Questa barzelletta, mi costerà due soldi). (*fa cenno ai giovani che dieno il rosolio*)

DON MARZIO (Oh questa poi della ballerina, voglio che tutti la sappiano).

RIDOLFO Servita del rosolio.

DON MARZIO Flusso, e riflusso, per la porta di dietro. (*bevendo il rosolio*)

RIDOLFO Ella starà male, quando ha il flusso, e riflusso per la porta di dietro.

SCENE VI

Enter RIDOLFO

RIDOLFO Sir.

DON MARZIO Since you don't know anything about the dancer, I'll tell you.

RIDOLFO To tell you the truth, I don't care for other people's business.

DON MARZIO But it's good to know something so that one knows how to act. She is protected by that scoundrel, Count Leandro. And from her earnings as a dancer, he takes the price of his protection. Instead of spending money on her, he eats up everything that poor wretch has. And because of him she's perhaps forced to do what she wouldn't otherwise do. What a rascal!

RIDOLFO But I'm here all day, and I can assure you that I've seen no one but Count Leandro go into her house.

DON MARZIO She has a backdoor, you idiot! In they come and out they go. She has a backdoor, you idiot!

RIDOLFO I mind my shop. Why should it matter to me if she has a backdoor? I don't stick my nose in anyone else's affairs.

DON MARZIO Scoundrel! You speak like this to someone of my station? (*stands*)

RIDOLFO I beg your pardon. Can't I make a joke?

DON MARZIO Give me a glass of rosolio.

RIDOLFO (*aside*) This joke is going to cost me a couple of farthings. (*gestures to the boys to pour Don Marzio the rosolio*)

DON MARZIO (*aside*) Oh, my! I'll let everyone know about the dancer.

RIDOLFO Here is your rosolio.

DON MARZIO (*drinking his rosolio*) In they come and out they go, through the backdoor.

RIDOLFO She must not be well with all this coming and going through the backdoor.

SCENA VII

EUGENIO *dalla bottega del giuoco, vestito da notte e stralunato, guardando il cielo e battendo i piedi; e detti*

DON MARZIO Schiavo, signor Eugenio.
EUGENIO Che ora è?
DON MARZIO Sedeci ore sonate.
RIDOLFO E il suo orologio va bene.
EUGENIO Caffè.
RIDOLFO La servo subito. (*va in bottega*)
DON MARZIO Amico, com'è andata?
EUGENIO Caffè. (*non abbadando a Don Marzio*)
RIDOLFO Subito. (*di lontano*)
DON MARZIO Avete perso? (*ad Eugenio*)
EUGENIO Caffè. (*gridando forte*)
DON MARZIO (Ho inteso, li ha persi tutti).
    (*va a sedere*)

SCENA VIII

PANDOLFO *dalla bottega del giuoco, e detti*

PANDOLFO Signor Eugenio, una parola. (*lo tira in disparte*)
EUGENIO So quel che volete dirmi. Ho perso trenta zecchini
    sulla parola. Son galantuomo, li pagherò.
pandolfo Ma il signor conte è là, che aspetta. Dice che ha
    esposto al pericolo i suoi denari, e vuol esser pagato.
DON MARZIO (Quanto pagherei a sentire che cosa dicono).
    (*da sé*)
RIDOLFO Ecco il caffè. (*ad Eugenio*)
EUGENIO Andate via. (*a Ridolfo*) Ha vinti cento zecchini in
    contanti; mi pare che non abbia gettata via la notte.
    (*a Pandolfo*)
PANDOLFO Queste non sono parole da giuocatore; V.S. sa
    meglio di me come va l'ordine in materia di giuoco.

SCENE VII

Enter EUGENIO *from the gambling house, in evening-dress and dazed, looking at the sky and stomping his feet*

DON MARZIO Your servant, Signor Eugenio.
EUGENIO What time is it?
DON MARZIO It's nine o'clock.
RIDOLFO And his watch runs fine.
EUGENIO Coffee.
RIDOLFO Right away, sir. (*enters the shop*)
DON MARZIO Friend, how did it go?
EUGENIO (*paying no attention to Don Marzio*) Coffee.
RIDOLFO (*from afar*) Right away.
DON MARZIO (*to Eugenio*) Did you lose?
EUGENIO (*yelling loudly*) Coffee.
DON MARZIO (*aside*) I understand. He lost everything.
    (*goes to sit down*)

SCENE VIII

Enter PANDOLFO *from the gambling house*

PANDOLFO Signor Eugenio, a word with you. (*takes him aside*)
EUGENIO I know what you want to tell me. I lost thirty sequins on my word. I'm a gentleman. I'll pay.
PANDOLFO But the Count is waiting. He says that he risked his money, and he wants to be paid.
DON MARZIO (*aside*) I'd give anything to hear what they're saying!
RIDOLFO (*to Eugenio*) Here's your coffee.
EUGENIO (*to Ridolfo*) Go away. (*to Pandolfo*) He won a hundred sequins in cash. It seems to me that he didn't waste the night.
PANDOLFO These are not the words of a gambler. You know the rules of gambling better than I, my lord.

RIDOLFO Signore, il caffè si raffredda. (*ad Eugenio*)

EUGENIO Lasciatemi stare. (*a Ridolfo*)

RIDOLFO Se non lo voleva . . .

EUGENIO Andate via.

RIDOLFO Lo beverò io. (*si ritira col caffè*)

DON MARZIO (Che cosa dicono?) (*a Ridolfo, che non gli risponde*)

EUGENIO So ancor io che, quando si perde, si paga, ma quando non ve n'è, non si può pagare. (*a Pandolfo*)

PANDOLFO Sentite, per salvare la vostra reputazione, son uomo capace di ritrovare trenta zecchini.

EUGENIO Oh bravo! Caffè. (*chiama forte*)

RIDOLFO Ora, bisogna farlo. (*ad Eugenio*)

EUGENIO Sono tre ore che domando caffè, e ancora non l'avete fatto?

RIDOLFO L'ho portato, ed ella mi ha cacciato via.

PANDOLFO Gliel'ordini con premura, che lo farà da suo pari.

EUGENIO Ditemi, vi dà l'animo di farmi un caffè, ma buono? Via, da bravo. (*a Ridolfo*)

RIDOLFO Quando mi dia tempo, la servo.
    (*va in bottega*)

DON MARZIO (Qualche grand'affare. Son curioso di saperlo).
    (*da sé*)

EUGENIO Animo, Pandolfo, trovatemi questi trenta zecchini.

PANDOLFO Io ho un amico che li darà; ma pegno e regalo.

EUGENIO Non mi parlate di pegno; che non facciamo niente. Ho que' panni a Rialto, che voi sapete, obbligherò que' panni, e quando gli venderò, pagherò.

DON MARZIO (Pagherò. Ha detto pagherò. Ha perso sulla parola). (*da sé*)

PANDOLFO Bene; che cosa vuol dar di regalo?

EUGENIO Fate voi quel che credete a proposito.

PANDOLFO Senta; non vi vorrà meno di un zecchino alla settimana.

EUGENIO Un zecchino di usura alla settimana?

RIDOLFO (*col caffè*) Servita del caffè. (*ad Eugenio*)

RIDOLFO (*to Eugenio*) Sir, the coffee is getting cold.
EUGENIO (*to Ridolfo*) Leave me alone.
RIDOLFO If you didn't want it . . .
EUGENIO Go away.
RIDOLFO Then I'll drink it. (*goes inside with the coffee*)
DON MARZIO (*to Ridolfo who doesn't answer*) What are they saying?
EUGENIO (*to Pandolfo*) I know full well that when you lose, you pay. But when you've run out, you can't pay.
PANDOLFO Listen. I'm the type of man who can find thirty sequins and save your reputation.
EUGENIO Great! (*calling out loudly*) Coffee.
RIDOLFO (*to Eugenio*) Oh dear, now I need to make it.
EUGENIO It's been three hours that I've been asking for coffee. And you still haven't made it?
RIDOLFO I brought it, and you chased me away.
PANDOLFO Order it from him nicely, and he'll make it like no one else.
EUGENIO (*to Ridolfo*) Tell me, can you find it in your heart to make me a good cup of coffee? There's a good fellow.
RIDOLFO If you give me a moment, I'll get it for you. (*goes into the shop*)
DON MARZIO (*aside*) Some important affair. I'm curious to find out what.
EUGENIO Come, come, Pandolfo. Find me the thirty sequins.
PANDOLFO I have a friend who can give you the money, but against security and with interest.
EUGENIO Don't talk to me about security, or we won't get anywhere. I have that cloth at Rialto, as you know. I'll put it up for sale, and when I sell it, I'll pay.
DON MARZIO (*aside*) "I'll pay." He said, "I'll pay." He lost on his word.
PANDOLFO Very well. How much interest do you want to pay?
EUGENIO You decide how much you believe is appropriate.
PANDOLFO Listen, it'll take at least a sequin a week.
EUGENIO A sequin of usury a week?
RIDOLFO (*with the coffee, to Eugenio*) Here's your coffee.

EUGENIO Andate via. (*a Ridolfo*)

RIDOLFO La seconda di cambio.

EUGENIO Un zecchino alla settimana? (*a Pandolfo*)

PANDOLFO Per trenta zecchini è una cosa discreta.

RIDOLFO Lo vuole, o non lo vuole? (*ad Eugenio*)

EUGENIO Andate via, che ve lo getto in faccia. (*a Ridolfo*)

RIDOLFO (Poveraccio! Il giuoco l'ha ubriacato). (*porta il caffè in bottega*)

DON MARZIO (*s'alza, e va vicino ad Eugenio*) Signor Eugenio, vi è qualche differenza? Volete che l'aggiusti io?

EUGENIO Niente, signor Don Marzio, la prego lasciarmi stare.

DON MARZIO Se avete bisogno, comandate.

EUGENIO Le dico, che non mi occorre niente.

DON MARZIO Messer Pandolfo, che avete voi col signor Eugenio?

PANDOLFO Un piccolo affare, che non abbiamo piacere di farlo sapere a tutto il mondo.

DON MARZIO Io sono amico del signor Eugenio, so tutti i fatti suoi, e sa che non parlo con nessuno. Gli ho prestati anche dieci zecchini sopra un paio d'orecchini; non è egli vero? e non l'ho detto a nessuno.

EUGENIO Si poteva anche risparmiare di dirlo adesso.

DON MARZIO Eh qui con messer Pandolfo si può parlare con libertà. Avete perso sulla parola? Avete bisogno di nulla? Son qui.

EUGENIO Per dirgliela, ho perso sulla parola trenta zecchini.

DON MARZIO Trenta zecchini, e dieci, che ve ne ho dati, sono quaranta; gli orecchini non possono valer tanto.

PANDOLFO Trenta zecchini, glieli troverò io.

DON MARZIO Bravo; trovategliene quaranta; mi darete i miei dieci, e vi darò i suoi orecchini.

EUGENIO (Maladetto sia quando mi sono impicciato con costui). (*da sé*)

DON MARZIO Perché non prendere il danaro, che vi offerisce il signor Pandolfo?
(*ad Eugenio*)

EUGENIO (*to Ridolfo*) Go away.

RIDOLFO And now a secondary exchange.

EUGENIO (*to Pandolfo*) A sequin a week?

PANDOLFO For thirty sequins, it seems fair to me.

RIDOLFO (*to Eugenio*) Do you want it, or don't you?

EUGENIO (*to Ridolfo*) Go away before I throw it in your face.

RIDOLFO (*aside*) Poor devil! He's drunk with gambling. (*takes the coffee into the back*)

DON MARZIO (*gets up and goes toward Eugenio*) Signor Eugenio, is there some misunderstanding? Do you want me to take care of it?

EUGENIO It's nothing, Signor Don Marzio. I beg you to leave me alone.

DON MARZIO If you are in need, feel free to call on me.

EUGENIO I tell you, I don't need anything.

DON MARZIO Master Pandolfo, what is your business with Signor Eugenio?

PANDOLFO A small matter that we prefer not to make known to the whole world.

DON MARZIO I am a friend of Signor Eugenio's. I know all about his affairs, and he knows that I don't gossip with anyone. I myself lent him ten sequins on a pair of earrings. Isn't that so? And I didn't tell anyone.

EUGENIO You didn't have to say so now.

DON MARZIO Oh, we can speak freely here with Master Pandolfo. Did you lose on your word? Are you in need of something? Here I am.

EUGENIO To tell the truth, I lost thirty sequins on my word.

DON MARZIO Thirty sequins, and ten that I gave you. That's forty. The earrings can't be worth that much.

PANDOLFO I'll find you the thirty sequins.

DON MARZIO Very well. Get him forty sequins. You'll give me my ten, and I'll give you his earrings.

EUGENIO (*aside*) Curse the hour that I got mixed up with this fellow!

DON MARZIO (*to Eugenio*) Why not take the money that Signor Pandolfo is offering you?

EUGENIO Perché vuole uno zecchino alla settimana.

PANDOLFO Io per me non voglio niente; è l'amico, che fa il servizio, che vuol così.

EUGENIO Fate una cosa; parlate col signor conte, ditegli che mi dia tempo ventiquattr'ore; son galantuomo, lo pagherò.

PANDOLFO Ho paura ch'egli abbia da andar via, e che voglia il denaro subito.

EUGENIO Se potessi vendere una pezza, o due di que' panni, mi spiccerei.

PANDOLFO Vuole che veda io di ritrovare il compratore?

EUGENIO Sì, caro amico, fatemi il piacere, che vi pagherò la vostra senseria.

PANDOLFO Lasci ch'io dica una parola al signor conte, e vado subito. (*entra nella bottega del giuoco*)

DON MARZIO Avete perso molto? (*ad Eugenio*)

EUGENIO Cento zecchini, che aveva riscossi ieri, e poi trenta sulla parola.

DON MARZIO Potevate portarmi i dieci, che vi ho prestati.

EUGENIO Via, non mi mortificate più; ve gli darò i vostri dieci zecchini.

PANDOLFO (*col tabarro e cappello dalla sua bottega*) Il signor conte si è addormentato colla testa sul tavolino. Intanto vado a veder di far quel servizio. Se si risveglia, ho lasciato l'ordine al giovane, che gli dica il bisogno. V.S. non si parta di qui.

EUGENIO Vi aspetto in questo luogo medesimo.

PANDOLFO (Questo tabarro è vecchio; ora è il tempo di farmene un nuovo a ufo). (*da sé; parte*)

SCENA IX

DON MARZIO *ed* EUGENIO, *poi* RIDOLFO

DON MARZIO Venite qui, sedete, beviamo il caffè.

EUGENIO Caffè. (*siedono*)

EUGENIO Because he wants a sequin a week.

PANDOLFO I don't want anything for myself. It's my friend who
performs the service that wants it.

EUGENIO Do this: speak with the Count. Tell him to give me
twenty-four hours. I'm a gentleman. I'll pay him.

PANDOLFO I'm afraid that he needs to be leaving, and he wants
the money right away.

EUGENIO If I could only sell a piece or two of that cloth, I
could get out of this predicament.

PANDOLFO Do you want me to see if I can find a buyer?

EUGENIO Yes, dear friend, do me this favor, and I will pay you
for your brokerage.

PANDOLFO Let me have a word with the Count. I'll go right
away. (*enters the gambling house*)

DON MARZIO (*to Eugenio*) Did you lose much?

EUGENIO One hundred sequins that I cashed yesterday, and
then thirty on my word.

DON MARZIO You could have brought me the ten that I lent you.

EUGENIO Come on, don't make it worse than it already is. I'll
give you your ten sequins.

(enter Pandolfo with cloak and hat, from his gambling house)

PANDOLFO The Count has fallen asleep with his head on the
table. In the meantime, I'll go see about this service. If he
wakes up, I left orders with the boy to tell him to wait. You
mustn't leave, my lord.

EUGENIO I'll wait for you right here.

PANDOLFO (*aside*) This cloak is old. Now it's time for me to get
a new one for free. *Exit Pandolfo*

SCENE IX

DON MARZIO Come, sit down. Let's drink some coffee.

EUGENIO Coffee. (*they sit*) (*enter Ridolfo*)

RIDOLFO A che giuoco giuochiamo, signor Eugenio? Si prende spasso de' fatti miei?

EUGENIO Caro amico, compatite, sono stordito.

RIDOLFO Eh caro signor Eugenio, se V.S. volesse badare a me, la non si troverebbe in tal caso.

EUGENIO Non so che dire, avete ragione.

RIDOLFO Vado a farle un altro caffè, e poi la discorreremo.
  (*si ritira in bottega*)

DON MARZIO Avete saputo della ballerina, che pareva non volesse nessuno? Il conte la mantiene.

EUGENIO Credo di sì, che possa mantenerla, vince gli zecchini a centinaia.

DON MARZIO Io ho saputo tutto.

EUGENIO Come l'avete saputo, caro amico?

DON MARZIO Eh, io so tutto. Sono informato di tutto. So quando vi va, quando esce. So quel che spende, quel che mangia; so tutto.

EUGENIO Il conte è poi solo?

DON MARZIO Oibò; vi è la porta di dietro.

RIDOLFO (*col caffè*) Ecco qui il terzo caffè.
  (*ad Eugenio*)

DON MARZIO Ah! Che dite, Ridolfo? So tutto io della ballerina?

RIDOLFO Io le ho detto un'altra volta, che non me ne intrico.

DON MARZIO Grand'uomo son io, per saper ogni cosa! Chi vuol sapere quel che passa in casa di tutte le virtuose e di tutte le ballerine, ha da venire da me.

EUGENIO Dunque questa signora ballerina è un capo d'opera.

DON MARZIO L'ho veramente scoperta come va. È robba di tutto gusto. Ah, Ridolfo, lo so io?

RIDOLFO Quando V.S. mi chiama in testimonio, bisogna ch'io dica la verità. Tutta la contrada la tiene per una donna da bene.

DON MARZIO Una donna da bene? Una donna da bene?

RIDOLFO Io le dico, che in casa sua non vi va nessuno.

DON MARZIO Per la porta di dietro, flusso, e riflusso.

RIDOLFO What game are we playing, Signor Eugenio? Do you find this amusing?

EUGENIO Dear friend, bear with me. I'm in a daze.

RIDOLFO Ah, dear Signor Eugenio, if you would listen to me, you wouldn't be in such a predicament.

EUGENIO I don't know what to say. You're right.

RIDOLFO I'm going to make you another coffee, and then we'll discuss it. *(enters the shop)*

DON MARZIO Have you heard about that dancer who seemed not to be interested in anyone? The Count looks after her.

EUGENIO I surely believe he can take care of her. He wins sequins by the hundreds.

DON MARZIO I found out all about it.

EUGENIO How did you find out, dear friend?

DON MARZIO Me? I know everything. I'm very well informed. I know when he goes there, when he leaves. I know what he spends, what he eats. I know everything.

EUGENIO So it's only the Count?

DON MARZIO Oh come, there's a backdoor.

RIDOLFO *(with the coffee, to Eugenio)* Here's your third coffee.

DON MARZIO Ah! What do you say, Ridolfo? Don't I know everything about the dancer?

RIDOLFO I told you once already that I'm not getting mixed up in this.

DON MARZIO I am quite a man for finding out everything. Whoever wants to know what goes on in the homes of actresses and dancers must come to me.

EUGENIO So, this dancer is a true gem.

DON MARZIO I've discovered what really goes on. It's quite refined stuff. Ridolfo, do I know or don't I?

RIDOLFO When you call me as witness, my lord, I have to tell the truth. All the neighborhood thinks her a respectable woman.

DON MARZIO A respectable woman? A respectable woman?

RIDOLFO I tell you that no one goes to her house.

DON MARZIO Through the backdoor, In they come and out they go.

EUGENIO E sì, ella pare una ragazza più tosto savia.

DON MARZIO Sì savia! Il conte Buonatesta la mantiene. Poi vi va chi vuole.

EUGENIO Io ho provato qualche volta a dirle delle paroline, e non ho fatto niente.

DON MARZIO Avete un filippo da scommettere? Andiamo.

RIDOLFO (Oh che lingua!) (*da sé*)

EUGENIO Vengo qui a bever il caffè ogni giorno; e per dirla non ho veduto andarvi nessuno.

DON MARZIO Non sapete che ha la porta segreta qui nella strada remota? Vanno per di là.

EUGENIO Sarà così.

DON MARZIO È senz'altro.

SCENA X

Il GARZONE *del barbiere, e detti*

GARZONE Illustrissimo, se vuol farsi far la barba, il padrone l'aspetta.
(*a Don Marzio*)

DON MARZIO Vengo. È così come io vi dico. Vado a farmi la barba, e come torno vi dirò il resto.
(*entra dal barbiere, e poi a tempo ritorna*)

EUGENIO Che dite, Ridolfo? La ballerina si è tratta fuori.

RIDOLFO Cred'ella al signor Don Marzio? Non sa la lingua ch'egli è?

EUGENIO Lo so che ha una lingua che taglia e fende. Ma parla con tanta franchezza, che convien dire che ei sappia quello che dice.

RIDOLFO Osservi, quella è la porta della stradetta. A star qui la si vede; e giuro da uomo d'onore, che per di là in casa non va nessuno.

EUGENIO Ma il conte la mantiene?

RIDOLFO Il conte va per casa, ma si dice che la voglia sposare.

EUGENIO And yet she seems a rather sensible girl.

DON MARZIO Sensible all right! Count Goodheart looks after her, and whoever wants to, goes there.

EUGENIO I've tried once or twice to have a little word with her, and I didn't get anywhere.

DON MARZIO Do you have a farthing to bet? Let's go and see.

RIDOLFO (aside) Oh, what a gossip!

EUGENIO I come here to have coffee every day, and, to tell the truth, I've seen no one go in there.

DON MARZIO Don't you know that she has a secret door on the street in back? That's how they get in.

EUGENIO If you say so.

DON MARZIO Of course it is.

SCENE X

Enter the barber's boy

BOY (to Don Marzio) Your grace, if you want to have a shave, my master is ready for you.

DON MARZIO I'm coming. It's as I tell you. I'm going to have a shave, and when I come back, I'll tell you the rest. (enters the barbershop)

EUGENIO What do you say, Ridolfo? The dancer has given herself away.

RIDOLFO Do you believe Signor Don Marzio? Don't you know what a gossip he is?

EUGENIO I know that he has a sharp and cutting tongue. But he speaks with such frankness that you have to assume he knows what he's talking about.

RIDOLFO Look. That's the alley door. From here you can see it, and I swear—as a man of honor—that no one goes into the house from there.

EUGENIO But is she kept by the Count?

RIDOLFO The Count goes to her house, but they say he wants to marry her.

EUGENIO Se fosse così, non vi sarebbe male; ma dice il signor
  Don Marzio che in casa vi va chi vuole.

RIDOLFO Ed io le dico che non vi va nessuno.

DON MARZIO (*esce dal barbiere col panno bianco al collo e la
  saponata sul viso*) Vi dico, che vanno per la porta di
  dietro.

GARZONE Illustrissimo, l'acqua si raffredda.

DON MARZIO Per la porta di dietro.
  (*entra dal barbiere col garzone*)

SCENA XI

EUGENIO *e* RIDOLFO

RIDOLFO Vede? È un uomo di questa fatta. Colla saponata sul
  viso.

EUGENIO Sì, quando si è cacciata una cosa in testa, vuole che
  sia in quel modo.

RIDOLFO E dice male di tutti.

EUGENIO Non so come faccia a parlar sempre de' fatti
  altrui.

RIDOLFO Le dirò: egli ha pochissime facoltà; ha poco da
  pensare a' fatti suoi, e per questo pensa sempre a
  quelli degli altri.

EUGENIO Veramente è fortuna il non conoscerlo.

RIDOLFO Caro signor Eugenio, come ha ella fatto a intricarsi
  con lui? Non aveva altri da domandare dieci zecchini in
  prestito?

EUGENIO Anche voi lo sapete?

RIDOLFO L'ha detto qui pubblicamente in bottega.

EUGENIO Caro amico, sapete come va: quando uno ha
  bisogno, si attacca a tutto.

RIDOLFO Anche questa mattina, per quel che ho sentito,
  V.S. si è attaccata poco bene.

EUGENIO Credete che messer Pandolfo mi voglia
  gabbare?

EUGENIO If it were so, there wouldn't be anything wrong. But Signor
Don Marzio says that whoever wants to goes to her house.
RIDOLFO And I tell you that no one goes there.
DON MARZIO (*comes out of the barber-shop with a towel around
his neck and lather on his face*) I tell you that they go
through the backdoor.
BOY Your grace, the water is getting cold.
DON MARZIO Through the backdoor. (*enters the barbershop with
the boy*)

SCENE XI

RIDOLFO You see? That's the kind of man he is. With lather on
his face.
EUGENIO Yes, when he gets something stuck in his head, there's
no stopping him.
RIDOLFO And he bad-mouths everyone.
EUGENIO I don't know how he can always speak of other
people's affairs.
RIDOLFO I'll tell you. He has few concerns. He spends little
time thinking about his own affairs, and so he's always
thinking about other people's.
EUGENIO You're really better off not knowing him.
RIDOLFO Dear Signor Eugenio, how could you get mixed up
with him? Wasn't there anyone else who could lend you ten
sequins?
EUGENIO You know about it too?
RIDOLFO He said so publicly, here in the shop.
EUGENIO Dear friend, you know how it goes: a man in need
will lay hold on anything.
RIDOLFO And this morning, from what I hear, my lord, you
didn't hold on too well.
EUGENIO Do you believe that Master Pandolfo wants to take
me in?

RIDOLFO Vedrà che razza di negozio le verrà a proporre.

EUGENIO Ma che devo fare? Bisogna che io paghi trenta zecchini, che ho persi sulla parola. Mi vorrei liberare dal tormento di Don Marzio. Ho qualche altra premura; se posso vendere due pezze di panno, fo tutti i fatti miei.

RIDOLFO Che qualità di panno è quello che vorrebbe esitare?

EUGENIO Panno padovano, che vale quattordici lire il braccio.

RIDOLFO Vuol ella che veda io di farglielo vendere con riputazione?

EUGENIO Vi sarei bene obbligato.

RIDOLFO Mi dia un poco di tempo, e lasci operare a me.

EUGENIO Tempo? volentieri. Ma quello aspetta i trenta zecchini.

RIDOLFO Venga qui, favorisca, mi faccia un ordine che mi sieno consegnate due pezze di panno, ed io medesimo le presterò i trenta zecchini.

EUGENIO Sì, caro, vi sarò obbligato. Saprò le mie obbligazioni.

RIDOLFO Mi maraviglio; non pretendo nemmeno un soldo. Lo farò per le obbligazioni ch'io ho colla buona memoria del suo signor padre, che è stato mio buon padrone, e dal quale riconosco la mia fortuna. Non ho cuor di vederla assassinare da questi cani.

EUGENIO Voi siete un gran galantuomo.

RIDOLFO Favorisca di stender l'ordine in carta.

EUGENIO Son qui; dettatelo voi, ch'io scriverò.

RIDOLFO Che nome ha il primo giovane del suo negozio?

EUGENIO Pasquino de' Cavoli.

RIDOLFO *Pasquino de' Cavoli . . .* (detta, ed Eugenio scrive) *Consegnerete a messer Ridolfo Gamboni . . . pezze due panno padovano . . . a sua elezione, acciò egli ne faccia esito per conto mio . . . avendomi prestato gratuitamente . . . zecchini trenta . . .* Vi metta la data, e si sottoscriva.

EUGENIO Ecco fatto.

RIDOLFO Si fida ella di me?

EUGENIO Capperi! Non volete?

RIDOLFO You'll see what kind of terms he'll propose.

EUGENIO But what am I to do? I need to pay thirty sequins
that I lost gambling on credit. I'd like to free myself from
Don Marzio's clutches. I have some other pressing matters.
If I can sell two bolts of cloth, all my affairs will be in
order.

RIDOLFO What quality of cloth is it that you'd like to dispose
of?

EUGENIO Paduan cloth, worth fourteen lire a yard.

RIDOLFO Do you want me to see if I can sell it for you for a
respectable sum?

EUGENIO I would be much obliged to you.

RIDOLFO Give me a little time, and let me work on it.

EUGENIO A little time? Gladly. But he's waiting on thirty
sequins.

RIDOLFO Come here please. Have two bolts of cloth delivered
to me, and I'll personally lend you the thirty sequins.

EUGENIO Yes, dear friend, I will be obliged to you. I shall
honor my obligations.

RIDOLFO You surprise me. I'm not asking for a penny. I'm
indebted to the memory of your worthy father, who was
my good master, and to whom I owe my good fortune. I
don't have the heart to see you killed by these dogs.

EUGENIO You are a true gentleman.

RIDOLFO Please draft me an order in writing.

EUGENIO I'm ready. You dictate, and I'll write.

RIDOLFO What's the name of the chap in charge of your store?

EUGENIO Pasquino de' Cavoli.

(*Ridolfo dictates and Eugenio writes*)

RIDOLFO Pasquino de' Cavoli . . . Deliver to Master Ridolfo
Gamboni . . . two bolts of Paduan cloth . . . as he may
select, in order that he may sell them for profit on my
behalf . . . having advanced to me without charge the sum
of thirty sequins . . . Put the date there and your signature.

EUGENIO It's done.

RIDOLFO Do you trust me?

EUGENIO Good Heavens! Shouldn't I?

RIDOLFO Ed io mi fido di lei. Tenga, questi sono trenta
zecchini. (*gli numera trenta zecchini*)

EUGENIO Caro amico, vi sono obbligato.

RIDOLFO Signor Eugenio, glieli do, acciò possa comparir
puntuale e onorato; le venderò il panno io, acciò non le
venga mangiato, e vado subito senza perder tempo; ma la
mi permetta che faccia con lei un piccolo sfogo d'amore,
per l'antica servitù che le professo. Questa, che V.S. tiene, è
la vera strada di andare in rovina. Presto presto si perde il
credito, e si fallisce. Lasci andar il giuoco, lasci le male
pratiche, attenda al suo negozio, alla sua famiglia, e si regoli
con giudizio. Poche parole, ma buone, dette da un uomo
ordinario, ma di buon cuore; se le ascolterà, sarà meglio per
lei. (*parte*)

SCENA XII

EUGENIO *solo, poi* LISAURA *alla finestra*

EUGENIO Non dice male; confesso che non dice male. Mia
moglie, povera disgraziata, che mai dirà? Questa notte non
mi ha veduto; quanti lunari avrà ella fatti? Già le donne,
quando non vedono il marito in casa, pensano cento cose,
una peggio dell'altra. Avrà pensato, o che io fossi con altre
donne, o che fossi caduto in qualche canale, o che per i
debiti me ne fossi andato. So che l'amore, ch'ella ha per me,
la fa sospirare; le voglio bene ancor io, ma mi piace la mia
libertà. Vedo però che da questa mia libertà ne ricavo più
mal che bene, e che se facessi a modo di mia moglie, le
faccende di casa mia andrebbero meglio. Bisognerà poi
risolversi, e metter giudizio. Oh quante volte ho detto
così! (*vede Lisaura alla finestra*) (Capperi! Grand'aria! Ho
paura di sì io, che vi sia la porticina col giuocolino).
Padrona mia riverita.

LISAURA Serva umilissima.

EUGENIO È molto, signora, che è alzata dal letto?

RIDOLFO And I trust you. Here, take these thirty sequins.
(*counts out thirty sequins*)

EUGENIO Dear friend, I am obliged to you.

RIDOLFO Signor Eugenio, I'm giving you the money so that you
can pay your debt on time and maintain your honor. I'll sell
the cloth for you so that it won't be squandered, and I'll do it
right away so as not to waste time. But permit me to speak a
loving word to you as an old servant of your house. The road
you're traveling, my lord, is the true road to ruin. Soon
enough you'll lose your credit and you'll go bankrupt. Forget
gambling. Forget your bad habits. Take care of your store
and of your family, and act with prudence. Just a few words
of advice from an ordinary yet goodhearted man. Heed these
words, and you'll be better off. (*exit Ridolfo*)

SCENE XII

EUGENIO He's right. I have to admit that he's right. My wife,
poor wretch, what will she say? Last night she didn't see
me. It must have made her crazy. Women. When their
husbands don't come home, they think a hundred different
things, each worse than the next. She probably thinks that I
was with other women, or that I fell into some canal, or
that I fled since I owe so much money. I know that she
worries because she loves me. I love her too, but I like my
freedom. I see, however, that it brings me more bad than
good and that if I did what she says, things at home would
get better. I've got to be resolute and set this right. Oh, how
many times have I said this! (*enter Lisaura at the window*)
Eugenio (*sees Lisaura at the window*) (*aside*) Faith! My stars!
Yes, I'm afraid that there is a little trick door. (*to Lisaura*)
My most reverend lady.

LISAURA Your most humble servant.

EUGENIO Has it been long, Signora, since you got up?

LISAURA In questo punto.

EUGENIO Ha bevuto il caffè?

LISAURA È ancora presto. Non l'ho bevuto.

EUGENIO Comanda che io la faccia servire?

LISAURA Bene obbligata. Non s'incomodi.

EUGENIO Niente, mi maraviglio; giovani, portate a quella
signora caffè, cioccolata; tutto quel ch'ella vuole.
Pago io.

LISAURA La ringrazio, la ringrazio. Il caffè e la cioccolata la
faccio in casa.

EUGENIO Avrà della cioccolata buona.

LISAURA Per dirla, è perfetta.

EUGENIO La sa far bene?

LISAURA La mia serva s'ingegna.

EUGENIO Vuole, che venga io, a darle una frullatina?

LISAURA È superfluo che s'incomodi.

EUGENIO Verrò a beverla con lei, se mi permette.

LISAURA Non è per lei, signore.

EUGENIO Io mi degno di tutto; apra, via, che staremo un'oretta
insieme.

LISAURA Mi perdoni, non apro con questa facilità.

eugenio Ehi, dica, vuole che io venga per la porta di
dietro?

LISAURA Le persone, che vengono da me, vengono
pubblicamente.

EUGENIO Apra, via, non facciamo scene.

LISAURA Dica in grazia, signore Eugenio, ha veduto ella il
conte Leandro?

EUGENIO Così non lo avessi veduto.

LISAURA Hanno forse giuocato insieme la scorsa notte?

EUGENIO Pur troppo; ma che serve che stiamo qui a far sentire
a tutti i fatti nostri? Apra, che le dirò ogni cosa.

LISAURA Vi dico, signore, che io non apro a nessuno.

EUGENIO Ha forse bisogno, che il signor conte le dia licenza?
Lo chiamerò.

LISAURA I got up just this moment.

EUGENIO Have you had your coffee?

LISAURA Not yet. It's still early.

EUGENIO May I see to it that you are served?

LISAURA Much obliged, but don't trouble yourself.

EUGENIO It's no trouble at all. Boys, bring the lady coffee, chocolate, all that she wants. I'm paying.

LISAURA Thank you. Thank you, but I make my coffee and chocolate at home.

EUGENIO You must have good chocolate.

LISAURA To tell the truth, it couldn't be better.

EUGENIO It's good, eh?

LISAURA My maid has a real knack for it.

EUGENIO Do you want me to come up and give it a little stir.

LISAURA You needn't trouble yourself.

EUGENIO With your permission, I'll come up and have some with you.

LISAURA It's not for you, sir.

EUGENIO I should be pleased to accept anything at all. Come now, open the door, and we'll spend a little while together.

LISAURA Forgive me, but I don't open the door so easily.

EUGENIO Well, tell me. Do you want me to come through the backdoor?

LISAURA People who come to my house have nothing to hide.

EUGENIO Come now, open the door. Let's not make a scene.

LISAURA Be so gracious to tell me, Signor Eugenio, have you seen Count Leandro?

EUGENIO I only wish I hadn't!

LISAURA Perhaps you played together last night?

EUGENIO Unfortunately. What good does it do us to make our affairs known to everyone? Open the door, and I'll tell you everything.

LISAURA I tell you, sir, that I don't open the door to anyone.

EUGENIO Perhaps you need the Count to give you permission? I'll call him.

LISAURA Se cerco del signor conte, ho ragione di farlo.

EUGENIO Ora la servo subito. È qui in bottega, che dorme.

LISAURA Se dorme, lasciatelo dormire.

SCENA XIII

LEANDRO, *dalla bottega del giuoco, e detti*

LEANDRO Non dormo no, non dormo. Son qui che godo la bella disinvoltura del signor Eugenio.

EUGENIO Che ne dite dell'indiscretezza di questa signora? Non mi vuole aprire la porta.

LEANDRO Chi vi credete che ella sia?

EUGENIO Per quel che dice Don Marzio, flusso, e riflusso.

LEANDRO Mente Don Marzio, e chi lo crede.

EUGENIO Bene. Non sarà così: ma col vostro mezzo non potrei io aver la grazia di riverirla?

LEANDRO Fareste meglio a darmi li miei trenta zecchini.

EUGENIO I trenta zecchini ve gli darò. Quando si perde sulla parola, vi è tempo a pagare ventiquattr'ore.

LEANDRO Vedete, signora Lisaura? Questi sono quei gran soggetti, che si piccano di onoratezza. Non ha un soldo, e pretende di fare il grazioso.

EUGENIO I giovani della mia sorta, signor conte caro, non sono capaci di mettersi in un impegno senza fondamento di comparir con onore. S'ella mi avesse aperto, non avrebbe perduto il suo tempo, e voi non sareste restato al di sotto coi vostri incerti. Questi sono danari, questi sono trenta zecchini, e queste faccie, quando non ne hanno, ne trovano. Tenete i vostri trenta zecchini, e imparate a parlare coi galantuomini della mia sorta.
(*va a sedere in bottega del caffè*)

LISAURA When I look for the Count, I have my own reasons
for doing so.
EUGENIO I'll get him for you right away. He's here in the
gambling house, sleeping.
LISAURA If he's sleeping, let him sleep.

SCENE XIII

Enter LEANDRO *from the gambling house*

LEANDRO I'm not sleeping. No, I'm not sleeping. I'm admiring
Signor Eugenio's savoir-faire.
EUGENIO What do you say of this lady's arrogance? She doesn't
want to open the door for me.
LEANDRO Who do you think she is?
EUGENIO According to Don Marzio, in they come and out
they go.
LEANDRO Don Marzio is a liar, and so is whoever believes him.
EUGENIO Well, maybe it's not so, but shall I not be able,
through your good offices, to pay her my respects?
LEANDRO You'd be better off paying me my thirty sequins.
EUGENIO I'll give you the thirty sequins. When you lose on
credit, you have twenty-four hours to pay.
LEANDRO Do you see, Signora Lisaura? He's one of those
characters who claim to be honorable. He doesn't have a
penny, and still thinks he's a charmer.
EUGENIO Young men of my kind, my dear Count, are not
capable of assuming an obligation without having the
means of discharging it with honor. Had she opened her
door to me, I wouldn't have wasted her time, and you
wouldn't have remained down here with your uncertainties.
This is money. This is thirty sequins, and these faces, when
they're not to be had, they're to be found. Take your thirty
sequins and learn how to speak with a gentleman like me.
(*goes to sit in the coffee house*)

LEANDRO (Mi ha pagato, dica ciò che vuole, che non m'importa). Aprite.
(*a Lisaura*)

LISAURA Dove siete stato tutta questa notte?

LEANDRO Aprite.

LISAURA Andate al diavolo.

LEANDRO Aprite. (*versa i zecchini nel cappello, acciò Lisaura li veda*)

LISAURA Per questa volta vi apro. (*si ritira ed apre*)

LEANDRO Mi fa grazia, mediante la raccomandazione di queste belle monete. (*entra in casa*)

EUGENIO Egli sì, ed io no? Non son chi sono, se non gliela faccio vedere.

SCENA XIV

PLACIDA *da pellegrina, ed* EUGENIO

PLACIDA Un poco di carità alla povera pellegrina.

EUGENIO (Ecco qui; corre la moda delle pellegrine). (*da sé*)

PLACIDA Signore, per amor del cielo, mi dia qualche cosa.
(*ad Eugenio*)

EUGENIO Che vuol dir questo, signora pellegrina? Si va così per divertimento, o per pretesto?

PLACIDA Né per l'un, né per l'altro.

EUGENIO Dunque per qual causa si gira il mondo?

PLACIDA Per bisogno.

EUGENIO Bisogno, di che?

PLACIDA Di tutto.

EUGENIO Anche di compagnia?

PLACIDA Di questa non avrei di bisogno, se mio marito non mi avesse abbandonata.

EUGENIO La solita canzonetta. Mio marito mi ha abbandonata. Di che paese siete, signora?

PLACIDA Piemontese.

EUGENIO E vostro marito?

LEANDRO (*aside*) He paid me. Let him say what he wants. I
    don't care. (*to Lisaura*) Open the door.
LISAURA Where were you all last night?
LEANDRO Open the door.
LISAURA Go to the devil.
LEANDRO Open the door. (*pours the sequins in his hat so that
    Lisaura sees them*)
LISAURA Just this once I'll open the door for you. (*goes inside
    and opens the door*)
LEANDRO She does me the favor—thanks to these bright coins.
    (*enters the house*)
EUGENIO Why him and not me? I'll show her what sort of man
    I am.

SCENE XIV

Enter PLACIDA *dressed as a wayfarer*

PLACIDA Charity for a poor wayfarer.
EUGENIO (*aside*) There you go. Wayfarers are in fashion.
PLACIDA (*to Eugenio*) Sir, for the love of Heaven, couldn't you
    give me a little something?
EUGENIO What do you mean by that, Signora? Are you merely
    amusing yourself, or have you come up with another excuse?
PLACIDA Neither the one, nor the other.
EUGENIO So what is it that makes you roam the world?
PLACIDA Because I need to.
EUGENIO What do you need?
PLACIDA Everything.
EUGENIO Even company?
PLACIDA I would have no need of that if my husband hadn't
    abandoned me.
EUGENIO The same old song: My husband abandoned me.
    Where are you from, Signora?
PLACIDA From Piedmont.
EUGENIO And your husband?

PLACIDA Piemontese egli pure.

EUGENIO Che facev'egli al suo paese?

PLACIDA Era scritturale d'un mercante.

EUGENIO E perché se n'è andato via?

PLACIDA Per poca volontà di far bene.

EUGENIO Questa è una malattia che l'ho provata anch'io, e non sono ancora guarito.

PLACIDA Signore, aiutatemi per carità. Sono arrivata in questo punto a Venezia. Non so dove andare; non conosco nessuno; non ho danari; son disperata.

EUGENIO Che cosa siete venuta a fare a Venezia?

PLACIDA A vedere se trovo quel disgraziato di mio marito.

EUGENIO Come si chiama?

PLACIDA Flaminio Ardenti.

EUGENIO Non ho mai sentito un tal nome.

PLACIDA Ho timore che il nome se lo sia cambiato.

EUGENIO Girando per la città, può darsi, che se vi è, lo troviate.

PLACIDA Se mi vedrà, fuggirà.

EUGENIO Dovreste far così. Siamo ora di carnovale, dovreste mascherarvi, e così più facilmente lo trovereste.

PLACIDA Ma come posso farlo, se non ho alcuno che mi assista? Non so nemmeno dove alloggiare.

EUGENIO (Ho inteso, or ora vado in pellegrinaggio ancor io). Se volete, questa è una buona locanda.

PLACIDA Con che coraggio ho da presentarmi alla locanda, se non ho nemmeno da pagare il dormire?

EUGENIO Cara pellegrina, se volete un mezzo ducato, ve lo posso dare. (Tutto quello che mi è avanzato dal giuoco). (*da sé*)

PLACIDA Ringrazio la vostra pietà. Ma più del mezzo ducato, più di qual si sia moneta, mi sarebbe cara la vostra protezione.

EUGENIO (Non vuole il mezzo ducato; vuole qualche cosa di più). (*da sé*)

PLACIDA He too is from Piedmont.

EUGENIO What did he do there?

PLACIDA He was a merchant's bookkeeper.

EUGENIO And why did he leave?

PLACIDA Little desire to do good.

EUGENIO I've suffered from this disease as well, and I'm not yet cured.

PLACIDA Sir, help me, in pity's name. I've just arrived in Venice. I don't know where to go. I don't know anyone. I don't have any money. I'm desperate.

EUGENIO Why did you come to Venice?

PLACIDA To see if I can find that no-good husband of mine.

EUGENIO What's his name?

PLACIDA Flaminio Ardenti.

EUGENIO I've never heard that name.

PLACIDA I'm afraid he's changed his name.

EUGENIO As you go about the city, if he's here, maybe you'll find him.

PLACIDA If he sees me, he'll flee.

EUGENIO Since it's now carnival, you should do this: wear a mask, and that way it will be easier to catch him.

PLACIDA But how can I do that if I don't have anyone to help me? I don't even know where I can find lodgings.

EUGENIO (*aside*) I understand. I'm about to do some way-faring of my own. (*to Placida*) If you'll permit me, this is a good inn.

PLACIDA How can I be so bold as to show myself at an inn if I don't have enough to pay for a bed?

EUGENIO My dear wayfarer, if you want a half-ducat, I can give it to you. (*aside*) It's all I have left from last night's game.

PLACIDA I thank you for your charity. But more than a half-ducat, more than any money, I would value your protection.

EUGENIO (*aside*) She doesn't want my half-ducat. She wants something more.

SCENA XV

DON MARZIO *dal barbiere, e detti*

DON MARZIO (Eugenio con una pellegrina! Sarà qualche cosa di buono!) (*siede al caffè guardando la pellegrina coll'occhialetto*)

PLACIDA Fatemi la carità; introducetemi voi alla locanda; raccomandatemi al padrone di essa, acciò, vedendomi così sola, non mi scacci, o non mi maltratti.

EUGENIO Volentieri. Andiamo, che vi accompagnerò; il locandiere mi conosce, e a riguardo mio, spero che vi userà tutte le cortesie che potrà.

DON MARZIO (Mi pare d'averla veduta altre volte). (*guarda di lontano coll'occhialetto*)

PLACIDA Vi sarò eternamente obbligata.

EUGENIO Quando posso, faccio del bene a tutti. Se non ritroverete vostro marito, vi assisterò io. Son di buon cuore.

DON MARZIO (Pagherei qualche cosa di bello a sentir cosa dicono).

PLACIDA Caro signore, voi mi consolate colle vostre cortesissime esibizioni. Ma la carità d'un giovine, come voi, ad una donna, che non è ancor vecchia, non vorrei che venisse sinistramente interpretata.

EUGENIO Vi dirò, signora: se in tutti i casi si avesse questo riguardo, si verrebbe a levare agli uomini la libertà di fare delle opere di pietà. Se la mormorazione è fondata sovra un'apparenza di male, si minora la colpa del mormoratore; ma se la gente cattiva prende motivo di sospettare da un'azion buona o indifferente, tutta la colpa è sua, e non si leva il merito a chi opera bene. Confesso d'esser anch'io uomo di mondo; ma mi picco insieme d'esser un uomo civile ed onorato.

PLACIDA Sentimenti d'animo onesto, nobile e generoso.

DON MARZIO Amico, chi è questa bella pellegrina? (*ad Eugenio*)

EUGENIO (Eccolo qui; vuol dar di naso per tutto). Andiamo in locanda. (*a Placida*)

PLACIDA Vi seguo. (*entra in locanda con Eugenio*)

SCENE XV

Enter DON MARZIO *from the barbershop*

DON MARZIO (*aside*) Eugenio with a wayfarer! This has got to be good! (*sits down at the cafe, looking at the wayfarer with his lorgnette*)

PLACIDA Do me this favor. Introduce me to the innkeeper. Speak a good word for me to him so that when he sees me like this, by myself, he won't chase me away or mistreat me.

EUGENIO Gladly. Let's go. I'll accompany you. The innkeeper knows me, and out of regard for me, I hope that he will extend you every courtesy.

DON MARZIO (*aside*) It seems to me that I've seen her before. (*looks on with the lorgnette*)

PLACIDA I will be eternally indebted to you.

EUGENIO I help everyone when I can. Should you not find your husband, I'll take care of you. I'm a goodhearted person.

DON MARZIO (*aside*) I'd pay something good to hear what they're saying.

PLACIDA Dear sir, you comfort me with your kind offer. But I wouldn't want the charity that a young man to be misinterpreted. After all, I am not yet an old woman.

EUGENIO Let me tell you, Signora. If everyone had such misgivings, a man's freedom to perform acts of kindness would be taken away. If a rumor is founded upon an apparent impropriety, the fault of the rumormonger is diminished. But if bad people find reason to suspect a good or indifferent action, the fault is totally theirs, and the merit is not taken away from those who act well. I confess that I'm no saint, but at the same time I pride myself on being a decent and honorable man.

PLACIDA These are the sentiments of an honest, noble and generous soul.

DON MARZIO (*to Eugenio*) Friend, who is this pretty wayfarer?

EUGENIO (*aside*) Here he goes again. He wants to stick his nose into everything. (*to Placida*) Let's go inside.

PLACIDA I'll follow you. (*enters the inn with Eugenio*)

SCENA XVI

DON MARZIO, *poi* EUGENIO *dalla locanda*

DON MARZIO Oh che caro signore Eugenio! Egli applica a
tutto, anche alla pellegrina. Colei mi pare certamente
sia quella dell'anno passato. Scommetterei, che è quella,
che veniva ogni sera al caffè, a domandar l'elemosina.
Ma io però non gliene ho mai dati veh! I miei danari,
che sono pochi, gli voglio spender bene. Ragazzi, non è
ancora tornato Trappola? Non ha portati gli orecchini,
che mi ha dati in pegno per dieci zecchini il signor
Eugenio?

EUGENIO Che cosa dice de' fatti miei?

DON MARZIO Bravo; colla pellegrina.

EUGENIO Non si può assistere una povera creatura, che si
ritrova in bisogno?

DON MARZIO Sì, anzi fate bene. Povera diavola!
Dall'anno passato in qua non ha trovato nessuno
che la ricoveri?

EUGENIO Come dall'anno passato! La conoscete quella
pellegrina?

DON MARZIO Se la conosco? E come! È vero che ho corta vista,
ma la memoria mi serve.

EUGENIO Caro amico, ditemi chi ella è.

DON MARZIO È una che veniva l'anno passato a questo caffè
ogni sera, a frecciare questo e quello.

EUGENIO Se ella dice che non è mai più stata in Venezia.

DON MARZIO E voi gliel'credete? Povero gonzo!

EUGENIO Quella dell'anno passato, di che paese era?

DON MARZIO Milanese.

EUGENIO E questa è piemontese.

DON MARZIO Oh, sì, è vero; era di Piemonte.

EUGENIO È moglie d'un certo Flamminio Ardenti.

DON MARZIO Anche l'anno passato aveva con lei uno, che
passava per suo marito.

EUGENIO Ora non ha nessuno.

SCENE XVI

DON MARZIO Oh, isn't he kind, Signor Eugenio! He gets
involved in everything, even that wayfarer. She certainly
seems to be the one from last year. I bet that she's the one
who used to come every evening to the cafe begging alms.
But I never gave her any! Hah. What little money I have, I
want to spend well. Boys, has Trappola come back yet?
Hasn't he brought back the earrings that Signor Eugenio
gave me as security for the ten sequins? *(enter Eugenio from
the inn)*

EUGENIO What are you saying about my affairs?

DON MARZIO Well. So now it's the wayfarer!

EUGENIO Can't I help a poor creature who finds herself in
need?

DON MARZIO Yes. Indeed, you do well to help her. Poor wretch!
Hasn't she found someone to give her shelter since last year?

EUGENIO What do you mean, since last year? Do you know
that wayfarer?

DON MARZIO Do I know her? I know her and how! It's true that
I'm short-sighted, but I have a good memory.

EUGENIO Dear friend, tell me who she is.

DON MARZIO Last year she used to come to this cafe every
evening to cozen one man or another.

EUGENIO And she told me that she had never been to Venice
before.

DON MARZIO And you believe her? You poor simpleton!

EUGENIO The one from last year, where was she from?

DON MARZIO Milan.

EUGENIO This one is from Piedmont.

DON MARZIO Oh, yes, you're right. From Piedmont.

EUGENIO She's the wife of a certain Flaminio Ardenti.

DON MARZIO Last year as well she had someone with her who
passed for her husband.

EUGENIO Now she doesn't have anyone.

DON MARZIO La vita di costoro; ne mutano uno al mese.

EUGENIO Ma come potete dire che sia quella?

DON MARZIO Se la conosco.

EUGENIO L'avete ben veduta?

DON MARZIO Il mio occhialetto non isbaglia; e poi l'ho sentita parlare.

EUGENIO Che nome avea quella dell'anno passato?

DON MARZIO Il nome poi non mi sovviene.

EUGENIO Questa ha nome Placida.

DON MARZIO Appunto; avea nome Placida.

EUGENIO Se fossi sicuro di questo, vorrei ben dirle quello che ella si merita.

DON MARZIO Quando dico una cosa io, la potete credere. Colei è una pellegrina, che invece d'essere alloggiata, cerca di alloggiare.

EUGENIO Aspettate, che ora torno. (Voglio sapere la verità).

(*entra in locanda*)

SCENA XVII

DON MARZIO, *poi* VITTORIA *mascherata*

DON MARZIO Non può esser altro che quella, assolutamente: l'aria, la statura, anche l'abito mi par quello. Non l'ho veduta bene nel viso, ma è quella senz'altro; e poi, quando mi ha veduto, subito si è nascosta nella locanda.

VITTORIA Signor Don Marzio, la riverisco. (*si smaschera*)

DON MARZIO Oh signora mascheretta, vi sono schiavo.

VITTORIA A sorte, avreste voi veduto mio marito?

DON MARZIO Sì, signora, l'ho veduto.

VITTORIA Mi sapreste dire dove presentemente egli sia?

DON MARZIO Lo so benissimo.

VITTORIA Vi supplico dirmelo per cortesia.

DON MARZIO What a life they lead! They change husbands
every month.

EUGENIO But how can you say that it's the same one?

DON MARZIO I know her!

EUGENIO Did you get a good look at her?

DON MARZIO My lorgnette is never mistaken, and I also heard
her speak.

EUGENIO What was the name of the one from last year?

DON MARZIO I don't remember her name.

EUGENIO This one is called Placida.

DON MARZIO That's right. She was called Placida.

EUGENIO If I were sure of this, I'd really like to tell her what she
deserves.

DON MARZIO When I say something, you can believe it. She's a
wayfarer all right, not so much seeking to be put up for the
night as to put one over on you.

EUGENIO Wait. I'll be right back. (*aside*) I want to find out the
truth. (*enters the inn*)

SCENE XVII

DON MARZIO It can't be anyone else but her, absolutely: her air,
her stature, even her dress seems the same. I didn't see her
face very well, but it's her without a doubt. And then, when
she saw me, she hid herself right away in the inn.
(*enter Vittoria with mask*)

VITTORIA Signor Don Marzio, my respects. (*takes off her mask*)

DON MARZIO I'm your servant, my sweet mask.

VITTORIA By chance, have you seen my husband?

DON MARZIO Yes, Signora, I've seen him.

VITTORIA Could you tell where he is at present?

DON MARZIO I certainly could.

VITTORIA I pray that you will have the kindness to tell me.

DON MARZIO Sentite. (*la tira in disparte*) È qui in questa locanda con un pezzo di pellegrina; ma! co' fiocchi.

VITTORIA Da quando in qua?

DON MARZIO Or ora; in questo punto; è capitata qui una pellegrina, l'ha veduta, gli è piaciuta, ed è entrato subitamente nella locanda.

VITTORIA Uomo senza giudizio! Vuol perdere affatto la riputazione.

DON MARZIO Questa notte l'avrete aspettato un bel pezzo.

VITTORIA Dubitava gli fosse accaduta qualche disgrazia.

DON MARZIO Chiamate poca disgrazia, aver perso cento zecchini in contanti, e trenta sulla parola?

VITTORIA Ha perso tutti questi danari?

DON MARZIO Sì! Ha perso altro! Se giuoca tutto il giorno, e tutta la notte, come un traditore.

VITTORIA (Misera me! Mi sento strappar il cuore). (*da sé*)

DON MARZIO Ora gli converrà vendere a precipizio quel poco di panno, e poi ha finito.

VITTORIA Spero che non sia in istato di andar in rovina.

DON MARZIO Se ha impegnato tutto.

VITTORIA Mi perdoni; non è vero.

DON MARZIO Lo volete dire a me?

VITTORIA Io l'avrei a saper più di voi.

DON MARZIO Se ha impegnato a me . . . Basta. Son galantuomo, non voglio dir altro.

VITTORIA Vi prego dirmi che cosa ha impegnato. Può essere che io non lo sappia.

DON MARZIO Andate, che avete un bel marito.

VITTORIA Mi volete dire che cosa ha impegnato?

DON MARZIO Son galantuomo, non vi voglio dir nulla.

DON MARZIO Listen. (*takes her aside*) He's here at the inn with quite some wayfarer. Oh boy! With all the trimmings.

VITTORIA How long has he been in there?

DON MARZIO He just now arrived. A wayfarer was passing through. He saw her. He liked her, and he went straight into the inn.

VITTORIA What a reckless man! He wants to ruin his good name.

DON MARZIO Last night you must have waited for him for a good while.

VITTORIA I was afraid some misfortune had befallen him.

DON MARZIO Do you call losing a hundred sequins in cash and thirty on credit a misfortune?

VITTORIA He lost all that money?

DON MARZIO Yes! And more too! What do you expect if he plays all day and all night like a scoundrel?

VITTORIA (*aside*) Woe is me! I feel my heart breaking.

DON MARZIO Now he'll have to sell off at a sacrifice what little cloth he has, and that's the end of him.

VITTORIA I hope that he isn't about to go bankrupt.

DON MARZIO Well, he's pawned everything.

VITTORIA Pardon me, but it's not true.

DON MARZIO You're telling me?

VITTORIA I ought to know better than you.

DON MARZIO If he's pawned things with me . . . Enough of this. I am a gentleman. I won't say anymore.

VITTORIA I beg you to tell me what he's pawned. It might be something I don't know.

DON MARZIO Go on now. You have a fine husband.

VITTORIA Do you care to tell what it is that he has pawned.

DON MARZIO I'm a gentleman. I don't have anything more to tell you.

SCENA XVIII

TRAPPOLA *colla scatola degli orecchini, e detti*

TRAPPOLA Oh son qui; ha detto il gioielliere . . . (Uh!
   Che vedo! La moglie del signore Eugenio; non voglio
   farmi sentire).
DON MARZIO Ebbene cosa dice il gioielliere?
   (*piano a Trappola*)
TRAPPOLA Dice che saranno stati pagati più di dieci
   zecchini, ma che non glieli darebbe.
   (*piano a Don Marzio*)
DON MARZIO Dunque non sono al coperto?
   (*a Trappola*)
TRAPPOLA Ho paura di no. (*a Don Marzio*)
DON MARZIO Vedete le belle baronate che fa vostro marito?
   (*a Vittoria*) Egli mi dà in pegno questi orecchini per dieci
   zecchini, e non vagliono nemmeno sei.
VITTORIA Questi sono li miei orecchini.
DON MARZIO Datemi dieci zecchini, e ve li do.
VITTORIA Ne vagliono più di trenta.
DON MARZIO Eh trenta fichi! Siete d'accordo anche voi.
VITTORIA Teneteli fin a domani, ch'io troverò li dieci zecchini.
DON MARZIO Fin a domani? Oh non mi corbellate. Voglio
   andarli a far vedere da tutti i gioiellieri di Venezia.
VITTORIA Almeno, non dite che sono miei, per la mia
   riputazione.
DON MARZIO Che importa a me della vostra riputazione!
   Chi non vuol che si sappia, non faccia pegni.
   (*parte*)

SCENE XVIII

Enter TRAPPOLA *with the earring-case*

TRAPPOLA Oh, here I am. The jeweler said . . . (aside) Oh! What do I see? Signor Eugenio's wife. I don't want her to hear me.

DON MARZIO (*quietly to Trappola*) Well, what did the jeweler say?

TRAPPOLA (*quietly to Don Marzio*) He says that you may have paid more than ten sequins for them, but he'd never pay that much.

DON MARZIO (*to Trappola*) So I'm not covered?

TRAPPOLA (*to Don Marzio*) I'm afraid not.

DON MARZIO (*to Vittoria*) Do you see your husband's fine roguery? He pawns these earrings to me for ten sequins, and they're not even worth six.

VITTORIA These are my earrings.

DON MARZIO Give me ten sequins, and I'll give them to you.

VITTORIA They're worth more than thirty.

DON MARZIO Thirty figs! You must be in league with him.

VITTORIA Keep them until tomorrow, and I'll find the ten sequins.

DON MARZIO Until tomorrow? Don't mock me. I want to have them appraised by all the jewelers in Venice.

VITTORIA At least don't say that they are mine, for my reputation's sake.

DON MARZIO What do I care about your reputation? If you don't want such things known, don't pawn your valuables. (*exit Don Marzio*)

SCENA XIX

VITTORIA *e* TRAPPOLA

VITTORIA Che uomo indiscreto! incivile! Trappola, dov'è il
vostro padrone?

TRAPPOLA Non lo so; vengo ora a bottega.

VITTORIA Mio marito, dunque, ha giuocato tutta la notte?

TRAPPOLA Dove l'ho lasciato iersera, l'ho ritrovato questa
mattina.

VITTORIA Maladettissimo vizio! E ha perso cento e trenta
zecchini?

TRAPPOLA Così dicono.

VITTORIA Indegnissimo giuoco! E ora se ne sta con una
forastiera in divertimenti?

TRAPPOLA Signora sì, sarà con lei. L'ho veduto varie volte
girarle d'intorno; sarà andato in casa.

VITTORIA Mi dicono che questa forastiera sia arrivata
poco fa.

TRAPPOLA No signora; sarà un mese che la c'è.

VITTORIA Non è una pellegrina?

TRAPPOLA Oibò pellegrina; ha sbagliato, perché finisce in ina;
è una ballerina.

VITTORIA E sta qui alla locanda?

TRAPPOLA Signora no, sta qui in questa casa.
(*accennando la casa*)

VITTORIA Qui? Se mi ha detto il signor Don Marzio, ch'egli
ritrovasi in quella locanda con una pellegrina.

TRAPPOLA Buono! Anche una pellegrina?

VITTORIA Oltre la pellegrina, vi è anche la ballerina? Una di
qua, e una di là?

TRAPPOLA Sì signora; farà per navigar col vento sempre in
poppa. Orza e poggia, secondo soffia la tramontana,
o lo scirocco.

VITTORIA E sempre ha da far questa vita? Un uomo di quella
sorta, di spirito, di talento, ha da perdere così miseramente
il suo tempo, sacrificare le sue sostanze, rovinar la sua casa?

SCENE XIX

VITTORIA What an inconsiderate, uncouth man! Trappola, where is your master?

TRAPPOLA I don't know. I just got to the shop.

VITTORIA So my husband gambled the whole night long?

TRAPPOLA I found him this morning where I left him last night.

VITTORIA Accursed vice! And he lost one hundred and thirty sequins?

TRAPPOLA That's what they say.

VITTORIA Abominable plague! And now he's amusing himself with a stranger?

TRAPPOLA Yes ma'am. He's probably with her. I've seen him around her a good deal of late. Likely he's at her house.

VITTORIA They tell me that this stranger arrived not long ago.

TRAPPOLA No ma'am. She's been here for maybe a month.

VITTORIA She's not a wayfarer?

TRAPPOLA What? A wayfarer? I don't know how you could get it wrong. 'Wayfarer' and 'dancer' don't sound at all alike. She's a dancer.

VITTORIA And she's staying here at the inn?

TRAPPOLA No ma'am. (*indicating the house*) She stays in this house.

VITTORIA Here? But Signor Don Marzio told me that he's at the inn with the wayfarer!

TRAPPOLA Fine! A wayfarer too?

VITTORIA Besides the wayfarer there's a dancer? One here and one there?

TRAPPOLA Yes ma'am. Probably to keep sailing before the wind. Windward to leeward, depending on whether the wind is North or South.

VITTORIA Must he always lead a life like this? Does a spirited and talented man like that have to waste his time so miserably, sacrifice his possessions, wreck his house? And

Ed io l'ho da soffrire? Ed io mi ho da lasciar maltrattare senza risentirmi? Eh voglio esser buona, ma non balorda; non voglio che il mio tacere faciliti la sua mala condotta. Parlerò: dirò le mie ragioni, e se le parole non bastano, ricorrerò alla giustizia.

TRAPPOLA È vero, è vero. Eccolo, che viene dalla locanda.

VITTORIA Caro amico, lasciatemi sola.

TRAPPOLA Si serva pure, come più le piace.

(*entra nell'interno della bottega*)

SCENA XX

VITTORIA, *poi* EUGENIO *dalla locanda*

VITTORIA Voglio accrescere la di lui sorpresa, col mascherarmi. (*si maschera*)

EUGENIO Io non so quel ch'io m'abbia a dire, questa nega, e quel tien sodo. Don Marzio, so che è una mala lingua. A queste donne che viaggiano, non è da credere. Mascheretta? A buon'ora! Siete mutola? Volete caffè? Volete niente? Comandate.

VITTORIA Non ho bisogno di caffè, ma di pane. (*si smaschera*)

EUGENIO Come! Che cosa fate voi qui?

VITTORIA Eccomi qui strascinata dalla disperazione.

EUGENIO Che novità è questa? A quest'ora in maschera?

VITTORIA Cosa dite eh? Che bel divertimento! A quest'ora in maschera.

EUGENIO Andate subito a casa vostra.

VITTORIA Anderò a casa, e voi resterete al divertimento.

EUGENIO Voi andate a casa, ed io resterò dove mi piacerà di restare.

VITTORIA Bella vita, signor consorte.

EUGENIO Meno ciarle, signora, vada a casa, che farà meglio.

VITTORIA Sì, anderò a casa; ma anderò a casa mia, non a casa vostra.

EUGENIO Dove intendereste d'andare?

do I have to suffer this? And am I to let myself be mistreated without resenting it? I want to be good, but not stupid. I don't want my silence to encourage his misbehavior. I'll talk to him. I'll tell him what I think. And if words aren't enough, I'll go to court.

TRAPPOLA Quite so. Quite so. Here he comes from the inn.

VITTORIA Dear friend, leave me.

TRAPPOLA Be my guest, as you like.
    (*enters the back of the shop*)

SCENE XX

VITTORIA I will increase his surprise by putting the mask on again. (*puts the mask on*) (*enter Eugenio from the inn*)

EUGENIO I don't know what to say. She denies it, and he stands firm. I know Don Marzio is a scandalmonger, and these women who travel are not to be trusted. A mask! Good morning! Are you a mute? Would you like a coffee? If you'd like something, I'm at your service.

VITTORIA I don't need coffee, but I do need bread.
    (*takes off her mask*)

EUGENIO How in the world? What are you doing here?

VITTORIA I came out of sheer desperation.

EUGENIO What's this all about? Masked so early in the day?

VITTORIA What do you think of that? Some fun! A mask so early!

EUGENIO Go home right away.

VITTORIA I'll go home, and you'll stay here and amuse yourself.

EUGENIO You go home, and I'll stay where I like.

VITTORIA Nice life, my dear spouse!

EUGENIO Enough nonsense, Signora. Go home, and you'll be better off.

VITTORIA Yes, I'll go home, but I'll go to my house, not to your house.

EUGENIO Where do you intend to go?

VITTORIA Da mio padre, il quale nauseato de' mali trattamenti, che voi mi fate, saprà farsi render ragione del vostro procedere, e della mia dote.

EUGENIO Brava, signora, brava. Questo è il gran bene che mi volete, questa è la premura che avete di me e della mia riputazione.

VITTORIA Ho sempre sentito dire che crudeltà consuma amore. Ho tanto sofferto, ho tanto pianto; ma ora non posso più.

EUGENIO Finalmente che cosa vi ho fatto?

VITTORIA Tutta la notte al giuoco.

EUGENIO Chi vi ha detto che io abbia giuocato?

VITTORIA Me l'ha detto il signor Don Marzio, e che avete perduto cento zecchini in contanti, e trenta sulla parola.

EUGENIO Non gli credete, non è vero.

VITTORIA E poi, a' divertimenti con la pellegrina.

EUGENIO Chi vi ha detto questo?

VITTORIA Il signor Don Marzio.

EUGENIO (Che tu sia maladetto!) Credetemi, non è vero.

VITTORIA E di più impegnare la robba mia; prendermi un paio di orecchini, senza dirmi niente? Sono azioni da farsi ad una moglie amorosa, civile e onesta, come sono io?

EUGENIO Come avete saputo degli orecchini?

VITTORIA Me l'ha detto il signor Don Marzio.

EUGENIO Ah lingua da tanaglie!

VITTORIA Già dice il signor Don Marzio, e lo diranno tutti, che uno di questi giorni sarete rovinato del tutto; ed io, prima che ciò succeda, voglio assicurarmi della mia dote.

EUGENIO Vittoria, se mi voleste bene, non parlereste così.

VITTORIA Vi voglio bene anche troppo, e se non vi avessi amato tanto, sarebbe stato meglio per me.

EUGENIO Volete andare da vostro padre?

VITTORIA Sì, certamente.

EUGENIO Non volete più star con me?

VITTORIA Vi starò, quando avrete messo giudizio.

EUGENIO Oh, signora dottoressa, non mi stia ora a seccare. (*alterato*)

VITTORIA To my father's house. He'll be sick when he hears
how you've mistreated me. He'll know how to deal with
your doings and my dowry.

EUGENIO Well, well, Signora. This shows your great love for
me. This is how you care for me and my reputation.

VITTORIA I've always heard that cruelty is the death of love.
I've suffered so much. I've cried so much. But now I can't
take anymore.

EUGENIO Really, what have I done to you?

VITTORIA All night gambling.

EUGENIO Who told you that I was gambling?

VITTORIA Signor Don Marzio told me. And he also told me that
you lost a hundred sequins in cash and thirty on credit.

EUGENIO Don't believe him. It's not true.

VITTORIA And then, amusing yourself with the wayfarer.

EUGENIO Who told you this?

VITTORIA Signor Don Marzio.

EUGENIO (*aside*) Curse you, Don Marzio! (*to Vittoria*) Believe
me. It's not true.

VITTORIA And what's more, you pawned my things. Take my
earrings without telling me? Is this the way you treat a
loving, civil, and honest wife?

EUGENIO How did you find out about the earrings?

VITTORIA Signor Don Marzio told me.

EUGENIO He ought to have his tongue cut out!

VITTORIA Signor Don Marzio is saying it already, and so will everyone: one of these days you'll be completely ruined. And
before that happens, I want to make sure my dowry is safe.

EUGENIO Vittoria, if you loved me, you wouldn't talk like that.

VITTORIA I love you too much, and if I hadn't loved you so
much, I would have been better off.

EUGENIO Do you intend to go to your father's house?

VITTORIA Yes, I certainly do.

EUGENIO You don't want to be with me anymore?

VITTORIA I'll be with you when you get some sense into your
head.

EUGENIO (*angry*) Oh, spare me, Signora Know-it-all.

VITTORIA Zitto; non facciamo scene per la strada.

EUGENIO Se aveste riputazione, non verreste a cimentare vostro marito in una bottega da caffè.

VITTORIA Non dubitate, non ci verrò più.

EUGENIO Animo; via di qua.

VITTORIA Vado, vi obbedisco, perché una moglie onesta deve obbedire anche un marito indiscreto. Ma forse, forse sospirerete d'avermi, quando non mi potrete vedere. Chiamerete forse per nome la vostra cara consorte, quando ella non sarà in grado più di rispondervi e di aiutarvi. Non vi potrete dolere dell'amor mio. Ho fatto quanto fare poteva una moglie innamorata di suo marito. M'avete con ingratitudine corrisposto; pazienza. Piangerò da voi lontana, ma non saprò così spesso i torti che voi mi fate. V'amerò sempre, ma non mi vedrete mai più. (*parte*)

EUGENIO Povera donna! Mi ha intenerito. So che lo dice, ma non è capace di farlo; le andrò dietro alla lontana, e la piglierò colle buone. S'ella mi porta via la dote, son rovinato. Ma non avrà cuore di farlo. Quando la moglie è in collera, quattro carezze bastano per consolarla. (*parte*)

VITTORIA Be quiet. Let's not make a scene in the street.

EUGENIO If you cared for your reputation, you wouldn't come to chide your husband in a coffee house.

VITTORIA Don't worry, I won't come again.

EUGENIO Come on. Off with you.

VITTORIA I'll go. I'll obey you because an honest wife must obey even a wayward husband. But maybe you will long for me when you can't see me anymore. You'll invoke the name of your dear wife when she won't be able to answer you and help you. But yet you won't be able to complain about my love. I've done everything a wife who loves her husband can do. You've responded with ingratitude. So be it. I will cry away from you, but I can't conscience all the wrong that you do me. I will always love you, but you won't see me ever again. (*exit Vittoria*)

EUGENIO Poor woman! She's touched my heart. I know that she says she will, but she's not capable of doing it. I'll follow after her and wheedle her till I bring her around. If she takes away the dowry, I'm ruined. But she won't have the heart to do it. When your wife is vexed, a few caresses are enough to console her. (*exit Eugenio*)

ATTO SECONDO

SCENA I

RIDOLFO *dalla strada, poi* TRAPPOLA *dalla bottega interna*

RIDOLFO Ehi. Giovani, dove siete?

TRAPPOLA Son qui, padrone.

RIDOLFO Si lascia la bottega sola, eh?

TRAPPOLA Ero lì coll'occhio attento, e coll'orecchio in veglia.
 E poi, che volete voi che rubino? Dietro al banco non
 vien nessuno.

RIDOLFO Possono rubar le chicchere. So io che vi è
 qualcheduno, che si fa l'assortimento di chicchere,
 sgraffignandole una alla volta ai poveri bottegai.

TRAPPOLA Come quelli che vanno dove sono rinfreschi, per
 farsi provvisione di tazze e di tondini.

RIDOLFO Il signor Eugenio è andato via?

TRAPPOLA Oh se sapeste! È venuta sua moglie; oh che
 pianti! oh che lamenti! Barbaro, traditore, crudele!
 Un poco amorosa, un poco sdegnata. Ha fatto tanto, che lo
 ha intenerito.

RIDOLFO E dove è andato?

TRAPPOLA Che domande! Stanotte non è stato a casa,
 sua moglie lo viene a ricercare; e domandate dove
 è andato?

RIDOLFO Ha lasciato nessun ordine?

TRAPPOLA È tornato per la porticina di dietro, a dirmi che
 a voi si raccomanda per il negozio dei panni, perché
 non ne ha uno.

RIDOLFO Le due pezze di panno le ho vendute a tredici lire il
 braccio, ed ho tirato il denaro, ma non voglio ch'egli lo
 sappia; non glieli voglio dar tutti, perché se gli ha nelle
 mani, gli farà saltare in un giorno.

ACT TWO

SCENE I

Enter RIDOLFO *from the street*

RIDOLFO Boys, where are you? (*enter Trappola from the back of the coffee house*)

TRAPPOLA Here I am, Master.

RIDOLFO So, you leave the shop all alone?

TRAPPOLA I was there with ears open and eyes peeled.
And what is there to steal anyway? No one goes
behind the counter.

RIDOLFO They can steal the coffee-cups. I know for sure that
there's someone collecting cups, pinching them one by
one from poor shop owners.

TRAPPOLA Like those who go to parties to keep up their
supply of cups and saucers.

RIDOLFO Has Signor Eugenio left?

TRAPPOLA If you only knew! His wife came by. Oh, how
she cried and complained! Barbarian! Cruel traitor!
With a little affection and a little anger she managed
to soften him up.

RIDOLFO And where did he go?

TRAPPOLA What kind of question is that! Last night he didn't
go home, his wife comes here looking for him, and you ask
where did he go?

RIDOLFO Did he leave any instructions?

TRAPPOLA He came back through the backdoor and told me to
remind you about the cloth deal because he's flat broke.

RIDOLFO I sold the two bolts of cloth for thirteen lire a yard,
and I got the money. But I don't want him to know. I don't
want to give it all to him because if he gets his hands on it,
he'll spend it in one day.

TRAPPOLA Quando sa che gli avete, gli vorrà subito.

RIDOLFO Non gli dirò d'averli avuti, gli darò il suo bisogno, e mi regolerò con prudenza.

TRAPPOLA Eccolo, che viene. *Lupus est in fabula.*

RIDOLFO Cosa vuol dire questo latino?

TRAPPOLA Vuol dire: il lupo pesta la fava.
(*si ritira in bottega ridendo*)

RIDOLFO È curioso costui. Vuol parlare latino, e non sa nemmeno parlare italiano.

SCENA II

RIDOLFO *ed* EUGENIO

EUGENIO Ebbene, amico Ridolfo, avete fatto niente?

RIDOLFO Ho fatto qualche cosa.

EUGENIO So che avete avute le due pezze di panno; il giovine me lo ha detto. Le avete esitate?

RIDOLFO Le ho esitate.

EUGENIO A quanto?

RIDOLFO A tredici lire il braccio.

EUGENIO Mi contento; danari subito?

RIDOLFO Parte alla mano, e parte col respiro.

EUGENIO Oimè! Quanto alla mano?

RIDOLFO Quaranta zecchini.

EUGENIO Via, non vi è male. Datemeli, che vengono a tempo.

RIDOLFO Ma piano, signor Eugenio, V.S. sa pure che gli ho prestati trenta zecchini.

EUGENIO Bene, vi pagherete quando verrà il restante del panno.

RIDOLFO Questo, la mi perdoni, non è un sentimento onesto da par suo. Ella sa come l'ho servita, con prontezza, spontaneamente, senza interesse, e la mi vuol far aspettare?

TRAPPOLA When he finds out that you have it, he'll want it right away.

RIDOLFO I won't tell him that I got it all. I'll give him what he needs, and then I'll see what happens.

TRAPPOLA Here he comes. *Lupus est in fabula.*

RIDOLFO What's it mean, this Latin of yours?

TRAPPOLA It means: the wolf pestles the fava.

  (*withdraws to the shop laughing*)

RIDOLFO He's a strange one. He thinks he speaks Latin, and he doesn't even know how to speak his native tongue.

SCENE II

Enter EUGENIO

EUGENIO So, my friend Ridolfo, have you been able to do anything?

RIDOLFO I managed to do something.

EUGENIO I heard that you got the two bolts of cloth. The boy told me. Did you sell them?

RIDOLFO I sold them.

EUGENIO For how much?

RIDOLFO Thirteen lire a yard.

EUGENIO Not bad. Did you get all the money?

RIDOLFO Some in hand, some in time.

EUGENIO Oh, no! How much in hand?

RIDOLFO Forty sequins.

EUGENIO Well, that's not bad. Give it to me. It's just in the nick of time.

RIDOLFO Slow down, Signor Eugenio. My lord, you know full well that I lent you thirty sequins.

EUGENIO Very well. You'll get your money when the balance is paid.

RIDOLFO This sentiment, I'm sorry to say, does not become you. You know how I have served you: promptly, quickly,

Anch'io, signore, ho bisogno del mio.

EUGENIO Via, avete ragione. Compatitemi, avete ragione.
Tenetevi li trenta zecchini, e date quei dieci a me.

RIDOLFO Con questi dieci zecchini non vuol pagare il
signor Don Marzio? Non si vuol levar d'intorno
codesto diavolo tormentatore.

EUGENIO Ha il pegno in mano, aspetterà.

RIDOLFO Così poco stima V.S. la sua riputazione? Si vuol
lasciar malmenare dalla lingua d'un chiaccherone?
Da uno, che fa servizio apposta per vantarsi d'averlo
fatto, e che non ha altro piacere che metter in discredito
i galantuomini?

EUGENIO Dite bene, bisogna pagarlo. Ma ho io da restar senza
denari? Quanto respiro avete accordato al compratore?

RIDOLFO Di quanto avrebbe di bisogno?

EUGENIO Che so io? Dieci, o dodici zecchini.

RIDOLFO Servita subito; questi sono dieci zecchini, e quando
viene il signor Don Marzio, io recupererò gli orecchini.

EUGENIO Questi dieci zecchini che mi date, di qual ragione
s'intende che sieno?

RIDOLFO Gli tenga, e non pensi altro. A suo tempo
conteggeremo.

EUGENIO Ma quando tireremo il resto del panno?

RIDOLFO La non ci pensi. Spenda quelli, e poi qualche
cosa sarà; ma badi bene di spenderli a dovere, di
non gettarli.

EUGENIO Sì, amico, vi sono obbligato. Ricordatevi nel conto
del panno tenervi la vostra senseria.

RIDOLFO Mi maraviglio; fo il caffettiere, e non fo il sensale. Se
m'incomodo per un padrone, per un amico, non pretendo
di farlo per interesse. Ogni uomo è in obbligo di aiutar
l'altro quando può, ed io principalmente ho obbligo di
farlo con V.S., per gratitudine del bene che ho ricevuto dal
suo signor padre. Mi chiamerò bastantemente
ricompensato, se di questi denari, che onoratamente gli ho
procurati, se ne servirà per profitto della sua casa, per
risarcire il suo decoro e la sua estimazione.

and without self-interest. And you want to make me wait? I
too, sir, have my obligations.

EUGENIO Well, you're right. Bear with me. You're right. Keep
the thirty sequins, and give me ten.

RIDOLFO Don't you want to pay Signor Don Marzio with these
ten sequins? Don't you want to get that devil off your back?

EUGENIO He's got his security. He'll wait.

RIDOLFO My lord, is this all you care for your reputation? Why
should you let yourself be bullied by that gossipmonger
and his chatter, by one who helps others just so he can brag
about it, and who has no other pleasure in life than discrediting true gentlemen?

EUGENIO You're right. I've got to pay him. But must I remain
penniless? How much time did you give the buyer?

RIDOLFO How much do you need?

EUGENIO I don't know. Ten or twelve sequins.

RIDOLFO Right away, sir. Here are ten sequins, and when
Signor Don Marzio comes by, I'll get the earrings back.

EUGENIO This money you're giving me, what is to be the
understanding about it?

RIDOLFO Keep it, and don't worry anymore. In time
we'll settle.

EUGENIO But when will we cash in on the rest of the cloth?

RIDOLFO Don't worry about it. Spend the money, and then
we'll see. But be sure to spend it wisely. Don't throw
it away.

EUGENIO Yes, friend, I am obliged to you. Don't forget your
brokerage fee in the bill for the cloth.

RIDOLFO I don't understand. I'm a coffeemaker, not a broker.
If I go out of my way for my master, for a friend, I don't
expect anything out of it. Every man is obliged to help
another when he can, and I am obliged to do so with you
principally, my lord, in gratitude for the good I have
received from your father. I'll consider myself compensated
if this money—that I have honorably procured for you—is
used to profit your household, so that your dignity and
honor will be restored.

EUGENIO Voi siete un uomo molto proprio e civile; è peccato, che facciate questo mestiere; meritereste meglio stato e fortuna maggiore.

RIDOLFO Io mi contento di quello che il cielo mi concede, e non scambierei il mio stato con tanti altri, che hanno più apparenza, e meno sostanza. A me nel mio grado non manca niente. Fo un mestiere onorato, un mestiere nell'ordine degli artigiani, pulito, decoroso e civile. Un mestiere, che esercitato con buona maniera, e con riputazione, si rende grato a tutti gli ordini delle persone. Un mestiero reso necessario al decoro delle città, alla salute degli uomini, e all'onesto divertimento di chi ha bisogno di respirare. (*entra in bottega*)

EUGENIO Costui è un uomo di garbo; non vorrei però, che qualcheduno dicesse che è troppo dottore. In fatti per un caffettiere pare che dica troppo; ma in tutte le professioni vi sono degli uomini di talento e di probità. Finalmente non parla né di filosofia, né di mattematica: parla da uomo di buon giudizio; e volesse il cielo che io ne avessi tanto, quanto egli ne ha.

SCENA III

CONTE LEANDRO *di casa di Lisaura, ed* EUGENIO

LEANDRO Signor Eugenio, questi sono i vostri denari; eccoli qui tutti in questa borsa; se volete che ve gli renda, andiamo.

EUGENIO Son troppo sfortunato, non giuoco più.

LEANDRO Dice il proverbio: Una volta corre il cane, e l'altra la lepre.

EUGENIO Ma io sono sempre la lepre, e voi sempre il cane.

LEANDRO Ho un sonno, che non ci vedo. Son sicuro di non poter tenere le carte in mano; eppure per questo maladetto vizio non m'importa di perdere, purché giuochi.

EUGENIO Anch'io ho sonno. Oggi non giuoco certo.

EUGENIO You are a very upright and decent man. It's a pity that this is your profession. You deserve a higher station and a better lot than this.

RIDOLFO I am happy with what Heaven gives me, and I wouldn't trade places with many others who have more show, but less substance. I lack nothing in my station. I have a respectable profession in the order of trades. It's honest, dignified, and decent. It's a profession that serves all classes of men when it's done rightly and nobly. It's a profession necessary to the dignity of the city, for the health of men, and for the wholesome amusement of all those who need some respite. (*enters the shop*)

EUGENIO There goes a gallant man. I wouldn't want anyone to think him too smart, however. In fact, for a coffee house owner, it seems he talks too much. But in every profession there are talented and upright men. At least he doesn't talk of philosophy or mathematics. He speaks like a man of sound judgment. If Heaven only willed that I were as wise as he is.

SCENE III

Enter LEANDRO *from* LISAURA'S *house*

LEANDRO Signor Eugenio, here's your money, right here in this purse. If you want it back, let's go.

EUGENIO I'm out of luck. I'm not gambling anymore.

LEANDRO You know the proverb: sometimes the hound wins, sometimes the hare.

EUGENIO But I'm always the hare, and you're always the hound.

LEANDRO I'm so sleepy, I can't see straight. I'm sure I wouldn't even be able to hold my cards. Yet thanks to this accursed habit, I don't care if I lose—as long as I play.

EUGENIO I'm sleepy myself. I'm certainly not playing today.

LEANDRO Se non avete denari non importa, io vi credo.

EUGENIO Credete che sia senza denari? Questi sono zecchini; ma non voglio giuocare. (*mostra la borsa con gli dieci zecchini*)

LEANDRO Giuochiamo almeno una cioccolata.

EUGENIO Non ne ho volontà.

LEANDRO Una cioccolata per servizio.

EUGENIO Ma se vi dico . . .

LEANDRO Una cioccolata sola sola, e chi parla di giuocar di più, perda un ducato.

EUGENIO Via, per una cioccolata, andiamo. (Già Ridolfo non mi vede). (*da sé*)

LEANDRO (Il merlotto è nella rete). (*entra con Eugenio nella bottega del giuoco*)

SCENA IV

DON MARZIO, *poi* RIDOLFO *dalla bottega*

DON MARZIO Tutti gli orefici gioiellieri mi dicono che non vagliono dieci zecchini. Tutti si maravigliano che Eugenio m'abbia gabbato. Non si può far servizio; non do più un soldo a nessuno, se lo vedessi crepare. Dove diavolo sarà costui? Si sarà nascosto per non pagarmi.

RIDOLFO Signore, ha ella gli orecchini del signor Eugenio?

DON MARZIO Eccoli qui, questi belli orecchini non vagliono un corno; mi ha trappolato. Briccone! si è ritirato per non pagarmi; è fallito, è fallito.

RIDOLFO Prenda, signore, e non faccia altro fracasso; questi sono dieci zecchini, favorisca darmi i pendenti.

DON MARZIO Sono di peso? (*osserva coll'occhialetto*)

RIDOLFO Glieli mantengo di peso, e se calano, son qua io.

DON MARZIO Gli mettete fuori voi?

LEANDRO If you don't have any money, it doesn't matter. I'll take your word.

EUGENIO You think I don't have any money? (*showing him his purse*) Here are ten sequins, but I don't want to play.

LEANDRO Let's just play for a cup of chocolate.

EUGENIO I don't feel like it.

LEANDRO A cup of chocolate a hand.

EUGENIO But I told you . . .

LEANDRO Just one little cup of chocolate. Whoever suggests we play for anything more loses a ducat.

EUGENIO All right. For a cup of chocolate. Let's go. (*aside*) Ridolfo won't see me.

LEANDRO (*aside*) The bird is in the snare. (*enters the gambling house with Eugenio*)

SCENE IV

Enter DON MARZIO

DON MARZIO All the jewelers tell me that they're not worth ten sequins. All of them are amazed that Eugenio cheated me. That's what you get when you do someone a favor. I'm never giving a penny to anyone again, even if he's dying. Where the devil could he be? He's probably hiding so he doesn't have to pay me.
(*enter Ridolfo from the back of the shop*)

RIDOLFO Sir, do you have Signor Eugenio's earrings?

DON MARZIO Here they are. Fine earrings, not worth a straw. He tricked me, that cheater! He's hiding so he doesn't have to pay me. He's ruined. He's ruined.

RIDOLFO Here, sir. Don't make any more ruckus. Here are ten sequins. Please give me the earrings.

DON MARZIO (*examining the sequins with his lorgnette*) These coins, solid gold?

RIDOLFO I guarantee them. If they're not, I'm to blame.

DON MARZIO Are you putting them up for sale?

RIDOLFO Io non c'entro; questi sono denari del signor
Eugenio.

DON MARZIO Come ha fatto a trovare questi denari?

RIDOLFO Io non so i fatti suoi.

DON MARZIO Gli ha vinti al giuoco?

RIDOLFO Le dico, che non lo so.

DON MARZIO Ah, ora che ci penso, avrà venduto il panno.
Sì, sì, ha venduto il panno; gliel'ha fatto vendere
messer Pandolfo.

RIDOLFO Sia come esser si voglia, prenda i denari, e favorisca
rendere a me gli orecchini.

DON MARZIO Ve gli ha dati da sé il signor Eugenio, o ve gli ha
dati Pandolfo?

RIDOLFO Oh l'è lunga! Gli vuole, o non gli vuole?

DON MARZIO Date qua, date qua. Povero panno! L'avrà
precipitato.

RIDOLFO Mi dà gli orecchini?

DON MARZIO Gli avete da portar a lui?

RIDOLFO A lui.

DON MARZIO A lui o a sua moglie?

RIDOLFO O a lui, o a sua moglie. (*con impazienza*)

DON MARZIO Egli dov'è?

RIDOLFO Non lo so.

DON MARZIO Dunque gli porterete a sua moglie?

RIDOLFO Gli porterò a sua moglie.

DON MARZIO Voglio venire anch'io.

RIDOLFO Gli dia a me, e non pensi altro. Sono un
galantuomo.

DON MARZIO Andiamo, andiamo, portiamoli a sua moglie.
(*s'incamina*)

RIDOLFO So andarvi senza di lei.

DON MARZIO Voglio farle questa finezza. Andiamo, andiamo.
(*parte*)

RIDOLFO Quando vuole una cosa, non vi è rimedio. Giovani,
badate alla bottega. (*lo segue*)

RIDOLFO It has nothing to do with me. This is Signor
    Eugenio's money.

DON MARZIO Where on earth did he find this money?

RIDOLFO That is his affair, not mine.

DON MARZIO Did he win it gambling?

RIDOLFO I'm telling you, I don't know.

DON MARZIO Now that I think about it, he probably sold the
    cloth. Yes, yes. He sold the cloth. He had Master Pandolfo
    sell it for him.

RIDOLFO Have it your way, but take the money, and please give
    me the earrings.

DON MARZIO Did Signor Eugenio give it to you himself, or did
    Pandolfo give it to you?

RIDOLFO What difference does it make? Do you want the
    money or not?

DON MARZIO Give it here. Give it to me. Mistreated cloth. I'm
    sure he gave it away.

RIDOLFO Are you going to give me the earrings?

DON MARZIO Are you supposed to take them to him?

RIDOLFO Yes, to him.

DON MARZIO To him, or his wife?

RIDOLFO *(impatiently)* To him or to his wife.

DON MARZIO Where is he?

RIDOLFO I don't know.

DON MARZIO So you'll take them to his wife?

RIDOLFO I'll take them to his wife.

DON MARZIO I'm coming too.

RIDOLFO Give them to me, and don't worry. I'm a gentleman.

DON MARZIO *(leaving)* Let's go, let's go. We'll take them to
    his wife.

RIDOLFO I know how to get there by myself.

DON MARZIO I want to do her this favor. Let's go. Let's go.
    (exit Don Marzio)

RIDOLFO When he wants something, there's no two ways about
    it. Lads, watch the shop. *(exit Ridolfo)*

SCENA V

GARZONI *in bottega*, EUGENIO *dalla biscazza*

EUGENIO Maladetta fortuna! Gli ho persi tutti. Per una
cioccolata ho perso dieci zecchini. Ma l'azione che mi ha
fatto mi dispiace più della perdita. Tirarmi sotto, vincermi
tutti i denari, e poi non volermi credere sulla parola? Ora
sì, che son punto; ora sì, che darei dentro a giuocare,
fino a domani. Dica Ridolfo quel che sa dire; bisogna che
mi dia degli altri denari. Giovani, dov'è il padrone?

GARZONE È andato via in questo punto.

EUGENIO Dov'è andato?

GARZONE Non lo so, signore.

EUGENIO Maladetto Ridolfo! Dove diavolo sarà andato? Signor
conte, aspettatemi, che or ora torno. (*alla porta della bisca*)
Voglio veder se trovo questo diavolo di Ridolfo. (*in atto di
partire*)

SCENA VI

PANDOLFO *dalla strada, e detto*

PANDOLFO Dove, dove, signor Eugenio, così riscaldato?

EUGENIO Avete veduto Ridolfo?

PANDOLFO Io no.

EUGENIO Avete fatto niente del panno?

PANDOLFO Signor sì, ho fatto.

EUGENIO Via bravo; che avete fatto?

PANDOLFO Ho ritrovato il compratore del panno; ma con
che fatica! L'ho fatto vedere da più di dieci, e tutti lo
stimano poco.

EUGENIO Questo compratore quanto vuol dare?

PANDOLFO A forza di parole l'ho tirato a darmi otto lire al braccio.

EUGENIO Che diavolo dite? Otto lire al braccio? Ridolfo me ne
ha fatto vendere due pezze a tredici lire.

SCENE V

BOYS *in the coffee house, enter* EUGENIO *from the gambling house*

EUGENIO Curse my luck! I lost it all. For a cup of chocolate, I
lost ten sequins. But the way he treated me is harder to bear
than the loss. Drag me in there and win all that money, and
then refuse to credit my word? Now that's going too far. It
really is. Now I'll play until tomorrow even if it kills me.
Let Ridolfo say what he wants. He's got to give me more
money. Boys, where's your master?
BOY He just left.
EUGENIO Where did he go?
BOY I don't know, sir.
EUGENIO Accursed Ridolfo! Where the devil could he have
gone? (*toward the gambling house*) Signor Count, wait for
me. I'll be right back. (*about to leave*) I want to see if I can't
find that devil, Ridolfo.

SCENE VI

Enter PANDOLFO *from the street*

PANDOLFO Where, where are you going, Signor Eugenio, so
worked up?
EUGENIO Have you seen Ridolfo?
PANDOLFO No, I haven't.
EUGENIO Have you done anything about the cloth?
PANDOLFO Yes, sir, I have.
EUGENIO Great! What have you done?
PANDOLFO I found a buyer, but it wasn't easy! I showed it to more
than ten people, and none of them thought much of it.
EUGENIO How much is this buyer willing to give?
PANDOLFO I talked him in to giving me eight lire a yard.
EUGENIO What the devil are you saying? Eight lire a yard?
Ridolfo sold two bolts of it at thirteen lire.

PANDOLFO Denari subito?

EUGENIO Parte subito, e il resto con respiro.

PANDOLFO Oh che buon negozio! Col respiro! Io vi fo dare
tutti i denari un sopra l'altro. Tante braccia di panno, tanti
bei ducati d'argento veneziani.

EUGENIO (Ridolfo non si vede! Vorrei denari; son punto).

PANDOLFO Se avessi voluto vendere il panno a credenza,
l'avrei venduto anche sedici lire. Ma col denaro alla
mano, al dì d'oggi, quando si possono pigliare,
si pigliano.

EUGENIO Ma se costa a me dieci lire.

PANDOLFO Cosa importa perder due lire al braccio nel panno,
se avete i quattrini per fare i fatti vostri, e da potervi
ricattare di quel che avete perduto?

EUGENIO Non si potrebbe migliorare il negozio? Darlo per
il costo?

PANDOLFO Non vi è speranza di crescere un quattrinello.

EUGENIO (Bisogna farlo per necessità). Via, quel che s'ha
da fare, si faccia subito.

PANDOLFO Fatemi l'ordine per aver le due pezze di panno,
e in mezz'ora vi porto qui il denaro.

EUGENIO Son qui subito. Giovani, datemi da scrivere.
(*i garzoni portano il tavolino col bisogno per iscrivere*)

PANDOLFO Scrivete al giovine, che mi dia quelle due pezze
di panno che ho segnate io.

EUGENIO Benissimo, per me è tutt'uno. (*scrive*)

PANDOLFO (Oh che bell'abito, che mi voglio fare!) (*da sé*)

SCENA VII

RIDOLFO *dalla strada, e detti*

RIDOLFO (Il signor Eugenio scrive d'accordo con messer
Pandolfo. Vi è qualche novità). (*da sé*)

PANDOLFO (Non vorrei che costui mi venisse a interrompere sul
più bello). (*da sé, vedendo Ridolfo*)

PANDOLFO Cash down?

EUGENIO Part of it right away, and the rest in time.

PANDOLFO Some good deal! In time! I'm getting you all the money up front. The more yards of cloth, the more ducats of Venetian silver.

EUGENIO (*aside*) Ridolfo's not around! I could use the money. This has gone too far.

PANDOLFO Had I wanted to sell the cloth on credit, I could have sold it for sixteen lire. But with the money up front, these days, you've got to take what you can get.

EUGENIO But the cloth cost me ten lire.

PANDOLFO What does it matter if you lose two lire a yard as long as you have the money to take care of your affairs, and to make up what you've lost?

EUGENIO Wouldn't it be possible to get a better deal? Couldn't we sell it at cost?

PANDOLFO We can't hope to get a penny more.

EUGENIO (*aside*) I've no other choice. (*to Pandolfo*) All right, do what you need to right away.

PANDOLFO Make me an order for two bolts of cloth, and in half an hour I'll bring you the money.

EUGENIO I'm right with you. Boys, bring me something to write on. (*boys bring a small writing table and writing implements*)

PANDOLFO Write an order for your boy to give me the two bolts of cloth I picked out.

EUGENIO (*writing*) Very well. It's all the same to me.

PANDOLFO (*aside*) Oh, what a fine suit I'm going to have made!

SCENE VII

Enter RIDOLFO *from the street*

RIDOLFO (*aside*) Signor Eugenio is writing an agreement with Master Pandolfo. Something must have happened.

PANDOLFO (*aside, watching Ridolfo*) I wouldn't want him to spoil what I've got going.

RIDOLFO Signor Eugenio, servitor suo.

EUGENIO Oh, vi saluto. (*seguitando a scrivere*)

RIDOLFO Negozi, negozi, signor Eugenio? Negozi?

EUGENIO Un piccolo negozietto. (*scrivendo*)

RIDOLFO Posso esser degno di saper qualche cosa?

EUGENIO Vedete cosa vuol dire a dar la roba a credenza?
Non mi posso prevalere del mio; ho bisogno di denari,
e conviene ch'io rompa il collo ad altre due pezze
di panno.

PANDOLFO Non si dice, che rompa il collo a due pezze di
panno, ma che le venda, come si può.

RIDOLFO Quanto le danno al braccio?

EUGENIO Mi vergogno a dirlo. Otto lire.

PANDOLFO Ma i suoi quatrini un sopra l'altro.

RIDOLFO E V.S. vuol precipitar la sua roba così miseramente?

EUGENIO Ma se non posso fare ammeno. Ho bisogno di denari.

PANDOLFO Non è anche poco, da un'ora all'altra trovar i denari
che gli bisognano.

RIDOLFO Di quanto avrebbe di bisogno? (*ad Eugenio*)

EUGENIO Che? Avete da darmene?

PANDOLFO (Sta a vedere che costui mi rovina il negozio). (*da sé*)

RIDOLFO Se bastassero sei, o sette zecchini gli troverei.

EUGENIO Eh via! Freddure, freddure! Ho bisogno di denari. (*scrive*)

PANDOLFO (Manco male!) (*da sé*)

RIDOLFO Aspetti; quanto importeranno le due pezze di panno a
otto lire il braccio?

EUGENIO Facciamo il conto. Le pezze tirano sessanta braccia
l'una: due via sessanta, cento e venti. Cento e venti ducati
d'argento.

PANDOLFO Ma vi è poi la senseria da pagare.

RIDOLFO A chi si paga la senseria? (*a Pandolfo*)

PANDOLFO A me, signore, a me. (*a Ridolfo*)

RIDOLFO Benissimo. Cento e venti ducati d'argento, a lire otto
l'uno, quanti zecchini fanno?

EUGENIO Ogni undici, quattro zecchini. Dieci via undici,
cento e dieci, e undici cento e ventuno. Quattro via undici,
quarantaquattro. Quarantaquattro zecchini meno un

RIDOLFO Signor Eugenio, your servant.

EUGENIO (*continues to write*) Oh, how are you?

RIDOLFO Deep in business, Signor Eugenio? Deep in business?

EUGENIO (*writing*) Oh, just a small deal.

RIDOLFO Would you care to enlighten me?

EUGENIO You see what it means to sell the goods on credit? I can't avail myself of my own property. I need money, and so I'll have to sacrifice another two bolts of cloth.

PANDOLFO Don't say sacrifice two bolts of cloth when you're getting what you can for them.

RIDOLFO How much are they giving you a yard?

EUGENIO I'm ashamed to tell you. Eight lire.

PANDOLFO But all of his money up front.

RIDOLFO Why, my lord, do you want to unload your goods so cheaply?

EUGENIO But I have no choice! I need the money.

PANDOLFO It wasn't easy, but in an hour I found him the money he needs.

RIDOLFO (*to Eugenio*) How much do you need?

EUGENIO What? Do you have some to give me?

PANDOLFO (*aside*) I'll bet he's going to queer the deal yet.

RIDOLFO If all you needed was six or seven sequins, I'd find them.

EUGENIO Are you joking? I need real money. (*writes*)

PANDOLFO (*aside*) I'm glad we settled that.

RIDOLFO Wait. How much will the two bolts bring at eight lire a yard?

EUGENIO Let's see. There are sixty yards in each roll. Two times sixty is one hundred and twenty. One hundred and twenty silver ducats.

PANDOLFO But there's the brokerage to pay.

RIDOLFO (*to Pandolfo*) To whom does he pay the brokerage?

PANDOLFO (*to Ridolfo*) To me, sir, to me.

RIDOLFO Very well. One hundred and twenty silver ducats, at eight lire each. How many sequins does that make?

EUGENIO For every eleven, four sequins. Ten times eleven is one hundred and ten. Plus eleven is one hundred and twenty one. Four times eleven is forty-four. Forty-four

ducato. Quarantatre e quattordici lire, moneta
veneziana.

PANDOLFO Dica pure quaranta zecchini. I rotti vanno per la
senseria.

EUGENIO Anche i tre zecchini vanno ne' rotti?

PANDOLFO Certo; ma i denari subito.

EUGENIO Via, via, non importa. Ve gli dono.

RIDOLFO (Oh che ladro!) Faccia ora il conto, signor Eugenio,
quanto importano le due pezze di panno a tredici lire?

EUGENIO Oh importano molto più!

PANDOLFO Ma col respiro; e non può fare i fatti suoi.

RIDOLFO Faccia il conto.

EUGENIO Ora lo farò colla penna. *Cento e venti braccia, a
lire tredici il braccio. Tre via nulla; due via tre sei; un
via tre; un via nulla; un via due; un via uno; somma:
nulla; sei; due e tre cinque; uno. Mille cinquecento e
sessanta lire.*

RIDOLFO Quanti zecchini fanno?

EUGENIO Subito ve lo so dire. (*conteggia*) Settanta zecchini
e venti lire.

RIDOLFO Senza la senseria.

EUGENIO Senza la senseria.

PANDOLFO Ma aspettarli chi sa quanto. Val più una pollastra
oggi, che un cappone domani.

RIDOLFO Ella ha avuto da me: prima trenta zecchini, e poi dieci,
che fan quaranta, e dieci degli orecchini che ho ricuperati,
che sono cinquanta. Dunque ha avuto da me a quest'ora
dieci zecchini di più di quello che gli dà subito, alla mano,
un sopra l'altro, questo onoratissimo signor sensale.

PANDOLFO (Che tu sia maladetto!) (*da sé*)

EUGENIO È vero, avete ragione; ma adesso ho necessità di denari.

RIDOLFO Ha necessità di denari? Ecco i denari; questi sono
venti zecchini e venti lire, che formano il resto di settanta
zecchini e venti lire, prezzo delle cento e venti braccia di
panno, a tredeci lire il braccio, senza pagare un soldo di
senseria; subito, alla mano, un sopra l'altro, senza
ladronerie, senza scrocchi, senza bricconate da truffatori.

sequins, less a ducat. Forty-three, and fourteen lire, Venetian coin.

PANDOLFO Let's say forty sequins. I keep the small change for my brokerage.

EUGENIO Are three sequins small change?

PANDOLFO Certainly, but you get the money right away.

EUGENIO All right. All right. It doesn't matter. I'll give it to you.

RIDOLFO (*aside*) What a thief! (*to Eugenio*) Now let's see, Signor Eugenio. How much do the two bolts bring at thirteen lire?

EUGENIO They bring a lot more!

PANDOLFO But paid over time: you can't take care of your affairs.

RIDOLFO Figure it out.

EUGENIO Now I'll do it in pen. *One hundred and twenty yards, at thirteen a yard. Three times zero. Two times three is six. One times three. One times zero. One times two. One times one. The total is: zero; six; two and three makes five; one. One thousand, five hundred, sixty lire.*

RIDOLFO How many sequins does that make?

EUGENIO I'll tell you right away. (*counts*) Seventy sequins and twenty lire.

RIDOLFO Without the brokerage.

EUGENIO Without the brokerage.

PANDOLFO But who knows how long you'll have to wait. A bird in hand is worth two in the bush.

RIDOLFO I gave you: first thirty sequins, and then ten. That makes forty, and ten for the earrings that I got back. That's fifty. Well then, I've given you now ten sequins more than you get right away in cash, up front, from him, this most honorable Signor Broker.

PANDOLFO (*aside*) Curse you!

EUGENIO It's true. You're right. But I need the money now.

RIDOLFO You're in need of money? Here it is: here are twenty sequins and twenty lire that make up the rest of the seventy sequins and twenty lire, price of the one hundred and twenty yards of cloth at thirteen lire a yard, without paying any brokerage. Right away, in hand, up front, without thievery, without sponging, without any cheater's tricks.

EUGENIO Quand'è così, Ridolfo caro, sempre più vi ringrazio; straccio quest'ordine, e da voi, signor sensale, non mi occorre altro. (*a Pandolfo*)

PANDOLFO (Il diavolo l'ha condotto qui. L'abito è andato in fumo). Bene, non importa, avrò gettati via i miei passi.

EUGENIO Mi dispiace del vostro incomodo.

PANDOLFO Almeno da bevere l'acquavite.

EUGENIO Aspettate, tenete questo ducato. (*cava un ducato dalla borsa che gli ha dato Ridolfo*)

PANDOLFO Obbligatissimo. (Già vi cascherà un'altra volta). (*da sé*)

RIDOLFO (Ecco, come getta via i suoi denari). (*da sé*)

PANDOLFO Mi comanda altro? (*ad Eugenio*)

EUGENIO La grazia vostra.

PANDOLFO (Vuole?) (*gli fa cenno se vuol giuocare, in maniera che Ridolfo non veda*)

EUGENIO (Andate, che vengo). (*di nascosto egli pure a Pandolfo*)

PANDOLFO (Già se gli giuoca prima del desinare). (*va nella sua bottega, e poi torna fuori*)

EUGENIO Come è andata, Ridolfo? Avete veduto il debitore così presto? Vi ha dati subito gli denari?

RIDOLFO Per dirgli la verità, gli avevo in tasca sin dalla prima volta; ma io non glieli voleva dar tutti subito, acciò non gli mandasse male sì presto.

EUGENIO Mi fate torto a dirmi così; non sono già un ragazzo. Basta . . . dove sono gli orecchini?

RIDOLFO Quel caro signor Don Marzio, dopo aver avuti i dieci zecchini, ha voluto per forza portar gli orecchini colle sue mani alla signora Vittoria.

EUGENIO Avete parlato voi con mia moglie?

RIDOLFO Ho parlato certo; sono andato anch'io col signor Don Marzio.

EUGENIO Che dice?

RIDOLFO Non fa altro che piangere; poverina! Fa compassione.

EUGENIO Se sapeste come era arrabiata contro di me! Voleva andar da suo padre, voleva la sua dote, voleva far delle cose grandi.

EUGENIO When you put it that way, dear Ridolfo, I can't thank you enough. I'll rip up this order. (*to Pandolfo*) And I won't be needing anything from you, Signor Broker.

PANDOLFO (*aside*) The devil himself must have brought him here. There goes my new suit. (*to Eugenio*) Very well, it doesn't matter. The only thing I wasted was time.

EUGENIO I'm sorry for the trouble.

PANDOLFO At least a glass of brandy.

EUGENIO (*takes out a ducat from the bag that Ridolfo gave him*) Wait. Take this ducat.

PANDOLFO Much obliged. (*aside*) Well, I'll catch him yet.

RIDOLFO (*aside*) So that's how he throws his money away.

PANDOLFO Is there anything else that you need?

EUGENIO Just your good will.

PANDOLFO (*to Eugenio, making a gesture inviting him to play cards, unseen by Ridolfo*) What do you say?

EUGENIO (*secretly to Pandolfo*) You go ahead. I'll follow.

PANDOLFO (*aside*) I'll have him at it again before dinner. (*enters the gambling house*)

EUGENIO How did it go, Ridolfo? Have you already seen the debtor? Did he already give you the money?

RIDOLFO To tell you the truth, I had the money in my pocket from the beginning. But I didn't want to give it to you right away, so that you wouldn't squander it so quickly.

EUGENIO You are wrong to speak to me like that. I'm not a child anymore. Enough. . . . Where are the earrings?

RIDOLFO After I gave him the ten sequins, the ever-kind Signor Don Marzio insisted on taking the earrings to Signora Vittoria personally.

EUGENIO Did you speak with my wife?

RIDOLFO Of course I did. I went along with Signor Don Marzio.

EUGENIO What did she say?

RIDOLFO All she did was cry. Poor dear! It makes you feel sorry for her.

EUGENIO You should have seen how mad she was! She wanted to go back to her father. She wanted her dowry back. She wanted to stir things up in grand fashion.

RIDOLFO Come l'ha accomodata?

EUGENIO Con quattro carezze.

RIDOLFO Si vede che le vuol bene; è assai di buon cuore.

EUGENIO Ma quando va in collera, diventa una bestia.

RIDOLFO Non bisogna poi maltrattarla. È una signora nata
bene, allevata bene. M'ha detto, che s'io lo vedo, gli dica
che vada a pranzo a buon ora.

EUGENIO Sì, sì, ora vado.

RIDOLFO Caro signor Eugenio, la prego, badi al sodo, lasci
andar il giuoco; non si perda dietro alle donne; giacché
V.S. ha una moglie giovine, bella, e che gli vuol bene,
che vuol cercare di più?

EUGENIO Dite bene, vi ringrazio davvero.

PANDOLFO (*dalla sua bottega si spurga, acciò Eugenio lo senta
e lo guardi. Eugenio si volta. Pandolfo fa cenno che
Leandro l'aspetta a giuocare. Eugenio colla mano fa cenno
che anderà; Pandolfo torna in bottega, Ridolfo non se
ne avvede*)

RIDOLFO Io la consiglierei andar a casa adesso. Poco manca al
mezzo giorno. Vada, consoli la sua cara sposa.

EUGENIO Sì, vado subito. Oggi ci rivedremo.

RIDOLFO Dove posso servirla, la mi comandi.

EUGENIO Vi sono tanto obbligato. (*vorrebbe andare al giuoco,
ma teme che Ridolfo lo veda*)

RIDOLFO Comanda niente? Ha bisogno di niente?

EUGENIO Niente, niente. A rivedervi.

RIDOLFO Le son servitore. (*si volta verso la sua bottega*)

EUGENIO (*vedendo che Ridolfo non l'osserva, entra nella
bottega del giuoco*)

RIDOLFO How did you calm her down?

EUGENIO With a hug and a kiss.

RIDOLFO You can tell that she loves you. She's a goodhearted woman.

EUGENIO But when she gets angry, she's a fury.

RIDOLFO You shouldn't mistreat her so. She was born a lady, well-bred. She told me that if I saw you, I should tell you to get home early for dinner.

EUGENIO Yes, yes. I'm on my way.

RIDOLFO Dear Signor Eugenio, I beg you: stand firm. Forget gambling. Stop chasing after women. My lord, you already have a young and beautiful wife who loves you. What more could you want?

EUGENIO You're right. I am very grateful to you.

PANDOLFO, (*from his gambling house, coughs so that Eugenio looks at him; Eugenio turns around; Pandolfo gestures that Leandro is waiting to play cards; Eugenio gestures by hand that he'll go; Pandolfo goes back inside; Ridolfo doesn't notice*)

RIDOLFO I'd advise you to go home now. It's almost noon. Go and take care of your dear wife.

EUGENIO Yes. I'll go right away. I'll see you later.

RIDOLFO Whenever I may be of service, you have only to call on me.

EUGENIO (*wanting to gamble, but fearful that ridolfo might see him*) I am much obliged to you.

RIDOLFO May I do something for you? Do you need anything?

EUGENIO No, no. See you later.

RIDOLFO Your servant. (*turns toward his coffee house*)

EUGENIO (*seeing that Ridolfo is not watching him, enters the gambling house*)

SCENA VIII

RIDOLFO, *poi* DON MARZIO

RIDOLFO Spero un poco alla volta tirarlo in buona strada.
Mi dirà qualcuno; perché vuoi tu romperti il capo per
un giovine che non è tuo parente, che non è niente del
tuo? E per questo? Non si può voler bene a un amico?
Non si può far del bene a una famiglia, verso la quale
ho delle obbligazioni? Questo nostro mestiere ha
dell'ozio assai. Il tempo, che avanza, molti l'impiegano
o a giuocare, o a dir male del prossimo. Io l'impiego
a far del bene, se posso.

DON MARZIO Oh che bestia! Oh che bestia! Oh che asino!

RIDOLFO Con chi l'ha, signor Don Marzio?

DON MARZIO Senti, senti, Ridolfo, se vuoi ridere. Un medico
vuol sostenere che l'acqua calda sia più sana dell'acqua
fredda.

RIDOLFO Ella non è di quest'opinione?

DON MARZIO L'acqua calda debilita lo stomaco.

RIDOLFO Certamente rilassa la fibra.

DON MARZIO Cos'è questa fibra?

RIDOLFO Ho sentito dire che nel nostro stomaco vi sono due
fibre, quasi come due nervi, dalle quali si macina il cibo,
e quando queste fibre si rallentano, si fa una cattiva
digestione.

DON MARZIO Sì signore, sì signore; l'acqua calda rilassa il
ventricolo, e la sistole, e la diastole non possono triturare
il cibo.

RIDOLFO Come c'entra la sistole, e la diastole?

DON MARZIO Che cosa sai tu, che sei un somaro? Sistole,
e diastole sono i nomi delle due fibre, che fanno la
triturazione del cibo digestivo.

RIDOLFO (Oh che spropositi! Altro, che il mio Trappola!)
(*da sé*)

SCENE VIII

RIDOLFO Bit by bit I hope to get him on the right path. They'll say to me: Why do you want to break your back for a young man who isn't even a relative of yours, who has nothing to do with you? Well? Can't I care for a friend? Can't I help a family to which I am indebted? This profession of ours allows for plenty of leisure time. Many spend the extra time gambling, or gossiping. I use it to help others when I can.
(*enter Don Marzio*)

DON MARZIO Oh, what a blockhead! Oh, what a blockhead! Oh, what an ass!

RIDOLFO With whom are you cross, Signor Don Marzio?

DON MARZIO Listen to this, Ridolfo, if you want to laugh. I know a doctor who maintains that hot water is healthier to drink than cold water.

RIDOLFO Don't you share his opinion?

DON MARZIO Hot water weakens the stomach.

RIDOLFO It certainly relaxes the fiber.

DON MARZIO What is this fiber?

RIDOLFO I've heard that there are two fibers in our stomach, almost like two nerves, that grind food. And when these fibers slow down, it causes bad digestion.

DON MARZIO Yes sir. Yes sir. Hot water relaxes the ventricle, and the systole and the diastole can't chop the food.

RIDOLFO What do the systole and the diastole have to do with it?

DON MARZIO What do you know, you jack-ass? Systole and diastole are the names of the two fibers that do the grinding of the digestive food.

RIDOLFO (*aside*) Oh what nonsense! He's worse than my Trappola!

SCENA IX

LISAURA *alla finestra, e detti*

DON MARZIO Ehi? L'amica della porta di dietro. (*a Ridolfo*)

RIDOLFO Con sua licenza vado a badare al caffè. (*va nell'interno della bottega*)

DON MARZIO Costui è un asino, vuol serrar presto la bottega. Servitor suo, padrona mia. (*a Lisaura guardandola di quando in quando col solito occhialetto*)

LISAURA Serva umilissima.

DON MARZIO Sta bene?

LISAURA Per servirla.

DON MARZIO Quant'è che non ha veduto il conte Leandro?

LISAURA Un'ora in circa.

DON MARZIO È mio amico il conte.

LISAURA Me ne rallegro.

DON MARZIO Che degno galantuomo!

LISAURA È tutta sua bontà.

DON MARZIO Ehi. È vostro marito?

LISAURA I fatti miei, non li dico sulla finestra.

DON MARZIO Aprite, aprite, che parleremo.

LISAURA Mi scusi, io non ricevo visite.

DON MARZIO Eh via!

LISAURA No davvero.

DON MARZIO Verrò per la porta di dietro.

LISAURA Anche ella si sogna della porta di dietro? Io non apro a nessuno.

DON MARZIO A me non avete a dir così. So benissimo che introducete la gente per di là.

LISAURA Io sono una donna onorata.

DON MARZIO Volete che vi regali quattro castagne secche? (*le cava dalla tasca*)

LISAURA La ringrazio infinitamente.

DON MARZIO Sono buone, sapete. Le fo seccare io ne' miei beni.

LISAURA Si vede che ha buona mano a seccare.

SCENE IX

Enter LISAURA *at the window*

DON MARZIO (*to Ridolfo*) Look! It's our friend from the backdoor.

RIDOLFO With your permission, I'm going to see to the coffee.
(*enters the shop*)

DON MARZIO He's an ass. He won't stay in business very long.
(*to Lisaura, watching her now and then with his lorgnette*)
Your servant, my lady.

LISAURA Your most humble servant.

DON MARZIO Are you well?

LISAURA At your service.

DON MARZIO When did you last see Count Leandro?

LISAURA About an hour ago.

DON MARZIO The Count is a friend of mine.

LISAURA Glad to hear it.

DON MARZIO A true gentleman!

LISAURA It's very kind of you to say so.

DON MARZIO Say, is he your husband?

LISAURA I don't discuss my affairs at the window.

DON MARZIO Open the door. Open the door, and we'll talk.

LISAURA I beg your pardon. I don't receive guests.

DON MARZIO Oh come!

LISAURA No, really.

DON MARZIO I'll come through the backdoor.

LISAURA So, you've dreamt up a backdoor too? I open my door
for no one.

DON MARZIO You don't have to talk to me that way. I know full
well that you receive people through there.

LISAURA I am a respectable woman.

DON MARZIO May I offer you some dried chestnuts?
(*takes them out from his pocket*)

LISAURA I'm deeply grateful.

DON MARZIO They're good, you know. I dry them myself on
my estate.

LISAURA I can see that you've a good hand for drying.

DON MARZIO Perché?

LISAURA Perché ha seccato anche me.

DON MARZIO Brava! Spiritosa! Se siete così pronta a far le capriole, sarete una brava ballerina.

LISAURA A lei non deve premere che sia brava, o non brava.

DON MARZIO In verità, non me ne importa un fico.

SCENA X

PLACIDA *da pellegrina alla finestra della locanda, e detti*

PLACIDA (Non vedo più il signor Eugenio). (*da sé*)

DON MARZIO Ehi. Avete veduto la pellegrina?
       (*a Lisaura, dopo avere osservato Placida coll'occhialetto*)

LISAURA E chi è colei?

DON MARZIO Una di quelle del buon tempo.

LISAURA E il locandiere riceve gente di quella sorta?

DON MARZIO È mantenuta.

LISAURA Da chi?

DON MARZIO Dal signor Eugenio.

LISAURA Da un uomo ammogliato? Meglio!

DON MARZIO L'anno passato, ha fatto le sue.

LISAURA Serva sua. (*ritirandosi*)

DON MARZIO Andate via?

LISAURA Non voglio stare alla finestra, quando in faccia vi è una donna di quel carattere. (*si ritira*)

SCENA XI

PLACIDA *alla finestra*, DON MARZIO *nella strada.*

DON MARZIO Oh, oh, oh, questa è bella! La ballerina si ritira per paura di perdere il suo decoro! Signora pellegrina, la reverisco. (*coll'occhialetto*)

DON MARZIO Is that so?

LISAURA Why don't you go dry up yourself!

DON MARZIO I like a spirited woman! Since you like frolicking so much, you must be a good dancer.

LISAURA It's no concern of yours, whether I'm a good dancer or not.

DON MARZIO To tell the truth, I couldn't care less.

SCENE X

Enter PLACIDA, *dressed as a wayfarer, at the window of the inn*

PLACIDA (*aside*) I don't see Signor Eugenio.

DON MARZIO (*to Lisaura, after looking at placida with his lorgnette*) Say, have you seen the wayfarer yet?

LISAURA Who is she?

DON MARZIO One of those women of pleasure.

LISAURA Does the innkeeper take in people like that?

DON MARZIO She's kept.

LISAURA By whom?

DON MARZIO By Signor Eugenio.

LISAURA A married man? Better yet!

DON MARZIO Last year she made the rounds.

LISAURA (*going back inside*) Your servant.

DON MARZIO Are you leaving?

LISAURA I don't want to be at the window when there's a woman of that sort across the way. (*goes back inside*)

SCENE XI

DON MARZIO Oh, oh, oh, this is grand! The dancer retires for fear of compromising her respectability! (*with his lorgnette*) Signora, my respects.

PLACIDA Serva devota.

DON MARZIO Dov'è il signore Eugenio?

PLACIDA Lo conosce ella il signore Eugenio?

DON MARZIO Oh siamo amicissimi. Sono stato poco fa a ritrovare sua moglie.

PLACIDA Dunque il signore Eugenio ha moglie?

DON MARZIO Sicuro, che ha moglie; ma ciò non ostante gli piace divertirsi coi bei visetti: avete veduto quella signora, che era a quella finestra?

PLACIDA L'ho veduta; mi ha fatto la finezza di chiudermi la finestra in faccia, senza fare alcun motto, dopo avermi ben bene guardata.

DON MARZIO Quella è una, che passa per ballerina, ma! M'intendete.

PLACIDA È una poco di buono?

DON MARZIO Sì; e il signore Eugenio è uno dei suoi protettori.

PLACIDA E ha moglie.

DON MARZIO E bella ancora.

PLACIDA Per tutto il mondo vi sono de' giovani scapestrati.

DON MARZIO Vi ha forse dato ad intendere che non era ammogliato?

PLACIDA A me poco preme che lo sia, o non lo sia.

DON MARZIO Voi siete indifferente. Lo ricevete com'è.

PLACIDA Per quello che ne ho da far io, mi è tutt'uno.

DON MARZIO Già si sa. Oggi uno, domani un altro.

PLACIDA Come sarebbe a dire? Si spieghi.

DON MARZIO Volete quattro castagne secche?
(*le cava di tasca*)

PLACIDA Bene obbligata.

DON MARZIO Davvero se volete, ve le do.

PLACIDA È molto generoso, signore.

DON MARZIO Veramente al vostro merito, quattro castagne sono poche. Se volete, aggiugnerò alle castagne un paio di lire.

PLACIDA Asino, senza creanza. (*serra la finestra e parte*)

DON MARZIO Non si degna di due lire, e l'anno passato si degnava di meno. Ridolfo. (*chiama forte*)

PLACIDA Your obedient servant.

DON MARZIO Where is Signor Eugenio?

PLACIDA Do you know Signor Eugenio?

DON MARZIO Oh, we're very good friends. I just went to call on his wife.

PLACIDA So, Signor Eugenio has a wife?

DON MARZIO Sure he has a wife. But that doesn't mean he doesn't like a pretty face. Did you see that lady at that window?

PLACIDA I saw her. She had the courtesy to close the window in my face, without a word, after she took a good look at me.

DON MARZIO She passes for a dancer, but . . . You understand.

PLACIDA Is she a loose woman?

DON MARZIO And Signor Eugenio is one of her protectors.

PLACIDA And he has a wife?

DON MARZIO And a pretty one at that.

PLACIDA The world is full of reckless youths.

DON MARZIO Perhaps he gave you reason to believe that he wasn't married?

PLACIDA I couldn't care less whether he is or not.

DON MARZIO You're indifferent. You take him as he is.

PLACIDA Insofar as it concerns me I don't care one way or the other.

DON MARZIO Yes, of course. One today, tomorrow another.

PLACIDA How do you mean? Explain yourself.

DON MARZIO Would you care for some dried chestnuts? (*takes them out of his pocket*)

PLACIDA Much obliged.

DON MARZIO Really, if you like, I'll give them to you.

PLACIDA You're too generous, sir.

DON MARZIO You're really worth more than a couple of chestnuts. If you want, I'll throw in a few lire.

PLACIDA You ill-mannered ass. (*closes the window*) (*exit Placida*)

DON MARZIO She's too good for a couple of lire . . . And to think last year she didn't mind less. (*calling out loudly*) Ridolfo!

SCENA XII

RIDOLFO e detto

RIDOLFO Signore?
DON MARZIO Carestia di donne. Non si degnano di due lire.
RIDOLFO Ma ella le mette tutte in un mazzo.
DON MARZIO Roba che gira il mondo? Me ne rido.
RIDOLFO Gira il mondo anche della gente onorata.
DON MARZIO Pellegrina! Ah, buffone!
RIDOLFO Non si può saper chi sia quella pellegrina.
DON MARZIO Lo so. È quella dell'anno passato.
RIDOLFO Io non l'ho più veduta.
DON MARZIO Perché sei un balordo.
RIDOLFO Grazie alla sua gentilezza. (Mi vien volontà di
    pettinargli quella parucca)

SCENA XIII

EUGENIO dal giuoco, e detti

EUGENIO Schiavo signori, padroni cari.
    (*allegro e ridente*)
RIDOLFO Come! Qui il signore Eugenio?
EUGENIO Certo; qui sono. (*ridendo*)
DON MARZIO Avete vinto?
EUGENIO Sì signore, ho vinto, sì signore.
DON MARZIO Oh! che miracolo!
EUGENIO Che gran caso! Non posso vincere io? Chi sono io?
    Sono uno stordito?
RIDOLFO Signor Eugenio, è questo il proponimento di non
    giuocare?
EUGENIO State zitto. Ho vinto.
RIDOLFO E se perdeva?
EUGENIO Oggi non potevo perdere.

SCENE XII

Enter RIDOLFO

RIDOLFO Sir?
DON MARZIO There's a shortage of women. They think they're too good for my money.
RIDOLFO What makes you think they're all the same?
DON MARZIO Just riffraff that roams the world. It makes me laugh.
RIDOLFO Respectable people roam the world too.
DON MARZIO A wayfarer! Ah, you fool!
RIDOLFO No one knows who that wayfarer is.
DON MARZIO I do. She's the one from last year.
RIDOLFO I've never seen her before.
DON MARZIO Because you're a numskull.
RIDOLFO Thanks for your kindness. (*aside*) I'd like to give that wig of his a brush or two.

SCENE XIII

Enter EUGENIO *from the gambling house*

EUGENIO (*happy and laughing*) Your servant, dear sirs and masters.
RIDOLFO How can it be! What's Signor Eugenio doing here?
EUGENIO (*laughing*) Of course I'm here.
DON MARZIO Did you win?
EUGENIO Yes sir, I won. Yes sir.
DON MARZIO It's a miracle!
EUGENIO What's the big deal? Can't I win too? Who do you think I am? A complete idiot?
RIDOLFO Signor Eugenio, is this your resolution to stop gambling?
EUGENIO Why don't you shut up. I won.
RIDOLFO What if you had lost?
EUGENIO I couldn't lose today.

RIDOLFO No? Perché?

EUGENIO Quando ho da perdere, me lo sento.

RIDOLFO E quando se lo sente, perché giuoca?

EUGENIO Perché ho da perdere.

RIDOLFO E a casa quando si va?

EUGENIO Via, mi principierete a seccare?

RIDOLFO Non dico altro. (Povere le mie parole!) (*da sé*)

SCENA XIV

LEANDRO *dalla bottega del giuoco, e detti*

LEANDRO Bravo, bravo; mi ha guadagnati li miei denari; e s'io non lasciava stare, mi sbancava.

EUGENIO Ah? Son uomo io? In tre tagli ho fatto il servizio.

LEANDRO Mette da disperato.

EUGENIO Metto da giuocatore.

DON MARZIO Quanto vi ha guadagnato?
       (*a Leandro*)

LEANDRO Assai.

DON MARZIO Ma pure, quanto avete vinto?
       (*ad Eugenio*)

EUGENIO Ehi; sei zecchini. (*con allegria*)

RIDOLFO (Oh pazzo maladetto! Da ieri in qua, ne ha perduti cento e trenta, e gli pare aver vinto un tesoro, ad averne guadagnati sei). (*da sé*)

LEANDRO (Qualche volta bisogna lasciarsi vincere per allettare). (*da sé*)

DON MARZIO Che volete voi fare di questi sei zecchini?
       (*ad Eugenio*)

EUGENIO Se volete che gli mangiamo, io ci sono.

DON MARZIO Mangiamoli pure.

RIDOLFO (Oh povere le mie fatiche!)

EUGENIO Andiamo all'osteria? Ognuno pagherà la sua parte.

RIDOLFO (Non vi vada, la tireranno a giuocare).
       (*piano ad Eugenio*)

RIDOLFO No? Why?

EUGENIO When I'm going to lose, I can feel it.

RIDOLFO And when you feel it, why do you play?

EUGENIO Because I've got to lose.

RIDOLFO And when are we going home?

EUGENIO Come off it. You're getting on my nerves.

RIDOLFO I've nothing more to say. (*aside*) Wasted words.

SCENE XIV

Enter LEANDRO *from the gambling house*

LEANDRO Congratulations. You've won my money. And if I
  didn't quit when I did, you would have cleaned me out.

EUGENIO Huh? That's the kind of man I am. I skinned you in
  three cuts.

LEANDRO You gamble like a madman.

EUGENIO I gamble like a skilled player.

DON MARZIO (*to Leandro*) How much did he win from you?

LEANDRO A lot.

DON MARZIO (*to Eugenio*) But really, how much did you win?

EUGENIO (*happily*) Six sequins.

RIDOLFO (*aside*) Accursed fool! Since yesterday he's lost one
  hundred and thirty, and he thinks he's won a fortune by
  earning six.

LEANDRO (*aside*) Every once in a while, you've got to let
  yourself be beaten to keep their hopes up.

DON MARZIO (*to Eugenio*) What are you going to do with these
  six sequins?

EUGENIO If you'd like to eat them, I'm for it.

DON MARZIO Let's eat them.

RIDOLFO (*aside*) All my efforts wasted.

EUGENIO Shall we go to the tavern? Everyone can pay for
  himself.

RIDOLFO (*quietly to Eugenio*) Don't go. They'll try to get you to
  play some more.

EUGENIO (Lasciateli fare; oggi sono in fortuna).
   (*piano a Ridolfo*)
RIDOLFO (Il male non ha rimedio). (*da sé*)
LEANDRO In vece di andare all'osteria, potremo far preparare
   qui sopra, nei camerini di messer Pandolfo.
EUGENIO Sì, dove volete; ordinaremo il pranzo qui alla
   locanda, e lo faremo portar là sopra.
DON MARZIO Io, con voi altri, che siete galantuomini, vengo
   per tutto.
RIDOLFO (Povero gonzo! Non se ne accorge). (*da sé*)
LEANDRO Ehi, messer Pandolfo.

SCENA XV

PANDOLFO *dal giuoco, e detti*

PANDOLFO Son qui a servirla.
LEANDRO Volete farci il piacere di prestarci i vostri stanzini per
   desinare?
PANDOLFO Son padroni; ma vede, anch'io . . . pago la
   pigione . . .
LEANDRO Si sa, pagheremo l'incomodo.
EUGENIO Con chi credete aver che fare? Pagheremo tutto.
PANDOLFO Benissimo; che si servano. Vado a far ripulire.
   (*va in bottega del giuoco*)
EUGENIO Via; chi va a ordinare?
LEANDRO Tocca a voi, come più pratico del paese. (*ad Eugenio*)
DON MARZIO Sì, fate voi. (*ad Eugenio*)
EUGENIO Che cosa ho da ordinare?
LEANDRO Fate voi.
EUGENIO Ma dice la canzone: L'allegria non è perfetta, quando
   manca la donnetta.
RIDOLFO (Anche di più vuol la donna!)
DON MARZIO Il signor conte potrebbe far venire la ballerina.
LEANDRO Perché no? In una compagnia d'amici non ho
   difficoltà di farla venire.

EUGENIO (*quietly to Ridolfo*) Let them try. I'm feeling lucky today.

RIDOLFO (*aside*) He's beyond all help.

LEANDRO Instead of going to the tavern, we could have them prepare something for us at Master Pandolfo's.

EUGENIO Fine, wherever you please. We'll order the dinner from the inn, and we'll have it brought upstairs.

DON MARZIO I'm with you, gentlemen, all the way.

RIDOLFO (*aside*) Poor simpleton! He doesn't know what he's getting into.

LEANDRO Hey, Master Pandolfo.

SCENE XV

Enter PANDOLFO *from the gambling house*

PANDOLFO Here I am, at your service.

LEANDRO Would you mind lending us your rooms for dinner?

PANDOLFO At your service, but, you see, I too . . . I pay rent . . .

LEANDRO Yes, of course. We'll pay you for your trouble.

EUGENIO Who do you think you're dealing with? We'll pay for everything.

PANDOLFO Very well, be my guest. I'll go have them prepared. (*enters the gambling house*)

EUGENIO So, who'll go order?

LEANDRO (*to Eugenio*) You should since you know the town.

DON MARZIO (*to Eugenio*) Yes, you do it.

EUGENIO What shall I order?

LEANDRO You decide.

EUGENIO How does the song go? Merriment is second-class, when a lad's without a lass.

RIDOLFO (*aside*) And he wants a woman too!

DON MARZIO The Count could have the dancer come.

LEANDRO Why not? I don't see any problem with her coming since we're all friends here.

DON MARZIO È vero, che la volete sposare? (*a Leandro*)

LEANDRO Ora non è tempo di parlare di queste cose.

EUGENIO Ed io vedrò di far venire la pellegrina.

LEANDRO Chi è questa pellegrina?

EUGENIO Una donna civile e onorata.

DON MARZIO (Sì, sì, l'informerò io di tutto). (*da sé*)

LEANDRO Via, andate a ordinare il pranzo.

EUGENIO Quanti siamo? Noi tre, due donne, che fanno cinque. Signor Don Marzio, avete dama?

DON MARZIO Io no. Son con voi.

EUGENIO Ridolfo, verrete anche voi a mangiare un boccone con noi.

RIDOLFO Le rendo grazie; io ho da badare alla mia bottega.

EUGENIO Eh via, non vi fate pregare.

RIDOLFO (Mi pare assai che abbia tanto cuore).
(*piano ad Eugenio*)

EUGENIO Che volete voi fare? Giacché ho vinto, voglio godere.

RIDOLFO E poi?

EUGENIO E poi, buona notte; all'avvenire ci pensan gli astrologhi. (*entra nella locanda*)

RIDOLFO (Pazienza! Ho gettata via la fatica).
(*si ritira*)

SCENA XVI

DON MARZIO *e il* CONTE LEANDRO

DON MARZIO Via, andate a prendere la ballerina.

LEANDRO Quando sarà preparato, la farò venire.

DON MARZIO Sediamo. Che cosa v'è di nuovo delle cose del mondo?

LEANDRO Io di nuove non me ne diletto. (*siedono*)

DON MARZIO Avete saputo che le truppe moscovite sono andate a quartiere d'inverno?

LEANDRO Hanno fatto bene; la stagione lo richiedeva.

DON MARZIO Signor no, hanno fatto male; non dovevano abbandonare il posto che avevano occupato.

DON MARZIO (*to Leandro*) Is it true that you want to marry her?
LEANDRO Now's not the time to speak of these things.
EUGENIO And I'll see if I can get the wayfarer to come.
LEANDRO Who is this wayfarer?
EUGENIO A decent and respectable lady.
DON MARZIO (*aside*) Yes, yes. I'll fill him in later.
LEANDRO Off with you. Go order the dinner.
EUGENIO How many are we? The three of us, and two women:
that makes five. Signor Don Marzio, do you have a lady?
DON MARZIO Not me. I'm with you.
EUGENIO Ridolfo, would you come have a bite to eat with us?
RIDOLFO Thank you. I have to look after my shop.
EUGENIO Come on, don't be shy.
RIDOLFO (*quietly to Eugenio*) I'm astonished you have such a
big heart.
EUGENIO What do you want me to do? I won, and I want to
enjoy it.
RIDOLFO And then?
EUGENIO And then, sweet dreams. Let the astrologers worry
about the future. (*enters the inn*)
RIDOLFO (*aside*) Oh well! I wasted my time.
(*withdraws*)

SCENE XVI

DON MARZIO Hurry up. Go fetch the dancer.
LEANDRO When everything's ready, I'll have her come.
DON MARZIO Let's sit down. What's new in the world?
LEANDRO I don't bother with the news.(*they sit*)
DON MARZIO Did you hear that the Muscovite troops went to
their winter quarters?
LEANDRO Good for them. The season called for it.
DON MARZIO No sir. It was a mistake. They shouldn't have
given up the place they had occupied.

LEANDRO È vero. Dovevano soffrire il freddo, per non perdere l'acquistato.

DON MARZIO Signor no; non avevano da arrischiarsi a star lì, con pericolo di morire nel ghiaccio.

LEANDRO Dovevano dunque tirare avanti.

DON MARZIO Signor no. Oh che bravo intendente di guerra! Marciar nella stagione d'inverno!

LEANDRO Dunque, che cosa avevano da fare?

DON MARZIO Lasciate ch'io veda la carta geografica, e poi vi dirò per l'appunto dove avevano a andare.

LEANDRO. (Oh che bel pazzo!)

DON MARZIO Siete stato all'opera?

LEANDRO Signor sì.

DON MARZIO Vi piace?

LEANDRO Assai.

DON MARZIO Siete di cattivo gusto.

LEANDRO Pazienza.

DON MARZIO Di che paese siete?

LEANDRO Di Torino.

DON MARZIO Brutta città.

LEANDRO Anzi passa per una delle belle d'Italia.

DON MARZIO Io sono napolitano. Vedi Napoli, e poi muori.

LEANDRO Vi darei la risposta del veneziano.

DON MARZIO Avete tabacco?

LEANDRO Eccolo. (*gli apre la scatola*)

DON MARZIO Oh che cattivo tabacco!

LEANDRO A me piace così.

DON MARZIO Non ve n'intendete. Il vero tabacco è il rapè.

LEANDRO A me piace il tabacco di Spagna.

DON MARZIO Il tabacco di Spagna è una porcheria.

LEANDRO Ed io dico che è il miglior tabacco che si possa prendere.

DON MARZIO Come! A me volete insegnare che cos'è tabacco? Io ne faccio, ne faccio fare, ne compro di qua, ne compro di là. So quel che è questo, so quel che è quello. Rapè, rapè vuol essere, rapè.
(*gridando forte*)

LEANDRO It's true. They should have suffered the cold rather
than lose the conquered territory.

DON MARZIO No sir. They didn't have to risk staying there with
the danger of freezing to death.

LEANDRO So they had to move on.

DON MARZIO No sir. Oh, you're a true war expert! To march in
the winter season!

LEANDRO So, what should they have done?

DON MARZIO Let me see a map, and then I'll tell you exactly
where they should have gone.

LEANDRO (*aside*) What a fool!

DON MARZIO Have you been to the opera?

LEANDRO Yes sir.

DON MARZIO Do you like it?

LEANDRO Very much so.

DON MARZIO You have bad taste.

LEANDRO Oh well.

DON MARZIO Where are you from?

LEANDRO Turin.

DON MARZIO An awful city.

LEANDRO On the contrary, it's one of Italy's most beautiful.

DON MARZIO I am Neapolitan. See Naples, and then you
can die.

LEANDRO I'd like to tell you what a Venetian would say.

DON MARZIO Do you have any snuff?

LEANDRO Here. (*opens the box for him*)

DON MARZIO Oh, what bad snuff!

LEANDRO I like it like this.

DON MARZIO You don't know snuff. Rappee is real snuff.

LEANDRO I like Spanish snuff.

DON MARZIO Spanish snuff is rubbish.

LEANDRO And I tell you it's the best snuff you can get.

DON MARZIO (*yelling loudly*) What? You want to teach me
what snuff is? I make snuff. I have it made. I buy it here,
I buy it there. I know what this kind is, and I know
what the other kind is too. Rappee, rappee, it has to
be rappee.

LEANDRO (*forte ancor esso*) Signor sì, rapè, rapè, è vero; il miglior tabacco è il rapè.

DON MARZIO Signor no. Il miglior tabacco non è sempre il rapè. Bisogna distinguere, non sapete quel che vi dite.

SCENA XVII

EUGENIO *ritorna dalla locanda, e detti*

EUGENIO Che è questo strepito?

DON MARZIO Di tabacco, non la cedo a nessuno.

LEANDRO Come va il desinare? (*ad Eugenio*)

EUGENIO Sarà presto fatto.

DON MARZIO Viene la pellegrina?

EUGENIO Non vuol venire.

DON MARZIO Via, signor dilettante di tabacco, andate a prendere la vostra signora.

LEANDRO Vado. (Se a tavola fa così, gli tiro un tondo nel mostaccio). (*picchia dalla ballerina*)

DON MARZIO Non avete le chiavi?

LEANDRO Signor no. (*gli aprono ed entra*)

DON MARZIO Avrà quelle della porta di dietro. (*ad Eugenio*)

EUGENIO Mi dispiace che la pellegrina non vuol venire.

DON MARZIO Farà per farsi pregare.

EUGENIO Dice che assolutamente non è più stata in Venezia.

DON MARZIO A me non lo direbbe.

EUGENIO Siete sicuro che sia quella?

DON MARZIO Sicurissimo; e poi, se poco fa ho parlato con lei, e mi voleva aprire . . . Basta, non sono andato, per non far torto all'amico.

EUGENIO Avete parlato con lei?

DON MARZIO E come!

EUGENIO Vi ha conosciuto?

DON MARZIO E chi non mi conosce? Sono conosciuto più della betonica.

LEANDRO (*yelling loudly*) Yes sir. Rappee, rappee. It's true. The best snuff is rappee.

DON MARZIO No, sir. The best snuff is not always rappee. You need to be discriminating. You don't know what you're talking about.

SCENE XVII

Enter EUGENIO *from the inn*

EUGENIO What's all this ruckus?

DON MARZIO On the subject of snuff, I yield to no one.

LEANDRO (*to Eugenio*) How's dinner coming?

EUGENIO It'll be ready soon.

DON MARZIO Is the wayfarer coming?

EUGENIO She doesn't want to come.

DON MARZIO Go on, Signor Snuff-amateur, go fetch your lady.

LEANDRO I'm going. (*aside*) If he does this at dinner, I'm going to throw a plate at that mug of his. (*knocks on the dancer's door*)

DON MARZIO Don't you have the keys?

LEANDRO No sir. (*the door is opened and Leandro enters*)

DON MARZIO (*to Eugenio*) He probably has the keys to the back door.

EUGENIO It's too bad that the wayfarer doesn't want to come.

DON MARZIO She just wants to hear you beg.

EUGENIO She says that she's absolutely never been to Venice.

DON MARZIO She wouldn't say that to me.

EUGENIO Are you sure it's her?

DON MARZIO Positive. And what's more, I spoke with her a while ago and she wanted me to come up . . . Of course, I didn't go, for friendship's sake.

EUGENIO You talked to her?

DON MARZIO Did I ever!

EUGENIO Did she recognize you?

DON MARZIO Who doesn't recognize me? My name is a household word.

EUGENIO Dunque fate una cosa. Andate voi a farla venire.

DON MARZIO Se vi vado io, avrà soggezione. Fate così; aspettate che sia in tavola; andatela a prendere, e senza dir nulla conducetela su.

EUGENIO Ho fatto quanto ho potuto, e m'ha detto liberamente che non vuol venire.

SCENA XVIII

CAMERIERI *di locanda che portano tovaglia, tovaglioli, tondini, posate, vino, pane, bicchieri e pietanze in bottega di Pandolfo, andando e tornando varie volte; poi* LEANDRO, LISAURA *e detti*

CAMERIERE Signori, la minestra è in tavola. (*va cogli altri in bottega del giuoco*)

EUGENIO IL CONTE DOV'È? (*a Don Marzio*)

DON MARZIO (*batte forte alla porta di Lisaura*) Animo, presto, la zuppa si fredda.

LEANDRO (*dando mano a Lisaura*) Eccoci, eccoci.

EUGENIO Padrona mia riverita. (*a Lisaura*)

DON MARZIO Schiavo suo. (*a Lisaura, guardandola coll'occhialetto*)

LISAURA Serva di lor signori.

EUGENIO Godo che siamo degni della sua compagnia. (*a Lisaura*)

LISAURA Per compiacere il signor conte.

DON MARZIO E per noi niente?

LISAURA Per lei particolarmente, niente affatto.

DON MARZIO Siamo d'accordo. (Di questa sorta di roba non mi degno). (*piano ad Eugenio*)

EUGENIO Via, andiamo, che la minestra patisce; resti servita. (*a Lisaura*)

LISAURA Con sua licenza. (*entra con Leandro nella bottega del giuoco*)

DON MARZIO Ehi! Che roba! Non ho mai veduta la peggio. (*ad Eugenio, col suo occhialetto, poi entra nella bisca*)

EUGENIO So you do it; go and get her to come.

DON MARZIO If I go, it might cause her embarrassment. Do this: wait until the food's on the table; go get her, and without saying anything, bring her up.

EUGENIO I did all I could, and she told me, frankly, that she doesn't want to come.

SCENE XVIII

Enter waiters from the inn carrying into PANDOLFO'S *a table-cloth, napkins, plates, utensils, wine, bread, glasses and food; they go back and forth a number of times*

WAITER Gentlemen, the soup is served. (*enters the gambling house with the others*)

EUGENIO (*to Don Marzio*) Where's the Count?

DON MARZIO (*knocking hard on lisaura's door*) Come, come. The soup's getting cold. (*enter Leandro and Lisaura*)

LEANDRO (*giving Lisaura his hand*) Here we are. Here we are.

EUGENIO (*to Lisaura*) My esteemed lady.

DON MARZIO (*to Lisaura, looking at her with his lorgnette*) Your servant.

LISAURA Your servant, gentlemen.

EUGENIO (*to Lisaura*) I'm happy that you find us worthy of your presence.

LISAURA Anything to please the Count.

DON MARZIO And nothing for us?

LISAURA Certainly not, especially not for you.

DON MARZIO Likewise, I'm sure. (*quietly to Eugenio*) I'm above all this.

EUGENIO Come, let's go. The soup's waiting. (*to Lisaura*) After you.

LISAURA With your permission. (*enters the gambling house with Leandro*)

DON MARZIO (*to Eugenio, with his lorgnette*) Can you believe this? I've never seen anything worse. (*enters the gambling house*)

EUGENIO Né anche la volpe non voleva le ciriegie. Io per altro mi degnerei. (*entra ancor esso*)

SCENA XIX

RIDOLFO *dalla bottega*

Eccolo lì, pazzo più che mai. A tripudiare con donne, e sua moglie sospira, e sua moglie patisce. Povera donna! Quanto mi fa compassione.

SCENA XX

EUGENIO, DON MARZIO, LEANDRO *e* LISAURA *nelli stanzini della biscaccia, aprono le tre finestre, che sono sopra le tre botteghe, ove sta preparato il pranzo, e si fanno vedere dalle medesime*

RIDOLFO *in istrada, poi* TRAPPOLA.

EUGENIO Oh che bell'aria! Oh che bel sole! Oggi non è niente freddo. (*alla finestra*)

DON MARZIO Pare propriamente di primavera. (*ad altra finestra*)

LEANDRO Qui almeno si gode la gente che passa.
    (*ad altra finestra*)

LISAURA Dopo pranzo vedremo le maschere. (*vicina a Leandro*)

EUGENIO A tavola, a tavola. (*siedono, restando Eugenio e Leandro vicini alla finestra*)

TRAPPOLA Signor padrone, che cos'è questo strepito? (*a Ridolfo*)

RIDOLFO Quel pazzo del signor Eugenio col signor Don Marzio, ed il conte colla ballerina, che pranzano qui sopra nei camerini di messer Pandolfo.

TRAPPOLA Oh bella! (*vien fuori, guarda in alto*) Buon pro a lor signori. (*verso le finestre*)

EUGENIO (*dalla finestra*) Trappola, evviva.

TRAPPOLA Evviva. Hanno bisogno d'aiuto?

EUGENIO Like the fox that didn't want the cherries. I, for one, wouldn't mind having them. (*enters the gambling house*)

SCENE XIX

Enter RIDOLFO *from the shop*

RIDOLFO There he is, crazier than ever. Making merry with women while his wife worries and suffers. Poor woman. I really feel sorry for her.

SCENE XX

EUGENIO, DON MARZIO, LEANDRO, *and* LISAURA *in the rooms of the gambling house where their meal has been prepared; they open the windows above the three shops and lean out*

EUGENIO (*at the window*) What wonderful air! What sunshine! Today it isn't cold at all.

DON MARZIO (*at another window*) It really feels like spring.

LEANDRO (*at another window*) From up here you certainly can enjoy the people passing by.

LISAURA (*near Leandro*) After dinner we'll see the masks.

EUGENIO Dinner is served, dinner is served. (*they sit, with Eugenio and Leandro near the windows*) (*enter Trappola*)

TRAPPOLA (*to Ridolfo*) Master, what's all this ruckus?

RIDOLFO That crazy Eugenio, Don Marzio, and the Count with the dancer are having dinner up there in Master Pandolfo's rooms.

TRAPPOLA (*comes out and looks up*) How nice! (*toward the window*) Bon appetit to all!

EUGENIO (*from the window*) Here's to Trappola.

TRAPPOLA Here's to you. Do you need any help?

EUGENIO Vuoi venire a dar da bere?

TRAPPOLA Darò da bere, se mi daranno da mangiare.

EUGENIO Vieni, vieni, che mangerai.

TRAPPOLA Signor padrone, con licenza. (*a Ridolfo; va per entrare nella bisca, ed un cameriere lo trattiene*)

CAMERIERE Dove andate? (*a Trappola*)

TRAPPOLA A dar da bere ai miei padroni.

CAMERIERE Non hanno bisogno di voi: ci siamo noi altri.

TRAPPOLA Mi è stato detto una volta, che oste in latino vuol dir nemico. Osti veramente nemici del pover'uomo!

EUGENIO Trappola, vieni su.

TRAPPOLA Vengo. A tuo dispetto. (*al cameriere ed entra*)

CAMERIERE Badate ai piatti, che non si attacchi sui nostri avanzi. (*entra in locanda*)

RIDOLFO Io non so come si possa dare al mondo gente di così poco giudizio! Il signore Eugenio vuole andare in rovina, si vuole precipitare per forza. A me, che ho fatto tanto per lui, che vede con che cuore, con che amore lo tratto, corrisponde così? Mi burla, mi fa degli scherzi? Basta: quel che ho fatto, l'ho fatto per bene, e del bene non mi pentirò mai.

EUGENIO Signor Don Marzio, e viva questa signora. (*forte, bevendo*)

TUTTI E viva, e viva.

SCENA XXI

VITTORIA *mascherata, e detti*

VITTORIA (*passeggia avanti la bottega del caffè, osservando se vi è suo marito*)

RIDOLFO Che c'è, signora maschera? che comanda?

EUGENIO Vivano i buoni amici. (*bevendo*)

VITTORIA (*sente la voce di suo marito, si avanza, guarda in alto, lo vede e smania*)

EUGENIO Would you like to come up and serve the wine?

TRAPPOLA I'll serve the wine if you give me something to eat.

EUGENIO Come up, come up and get some food.

TRAPPOLA (*to Ridolfo*) Master, with your permission. (*tries to enter the gambling house, and a waiter stops him*)

WAITER (*to Trappola*) Where are you going?

TRAPPOLA To serve wine to my masters.

WAITER They don't need you. We're here.

TRAPPOLA Someone once told me that host means enemy in Latin. Hostelry people certainly are hostile when it comes to the common man!

EUGENIO Trappola, come up.

TRAPPOLA Coming. (*to waiter*) With all due disrespect. (*enters the gambling house*)

WAITER Careful with the plates, and don't let him get his hands on our leftovers. (*enters the inn*)

RIDOLFO I don't know how there can be such senseless people in the world. Signor Eugenio is headed for ruin. He's bent on destroying himself. How can he talk like that to me, someone who's done so much for him, who treats him with a big heart and a lot of love? How can he laugh at me and make fun of me? I've had enough. I did what I did for the sake of good. And I'll never be sorry for that.

EUGENIO (*drinking, loudly*) Signor Don Marzio, here's to the lady.

ALL Cheers.

SCENE XXI

Enter VITTORIA, *masked, walking in front of the coffee house looking for her husband*

RIDOLFO What's the matter, masked lady? What can I do for you?

EUGENIO (*drinking*) Here's to good friends.

VITTORIA (*hears the voice of her husband, moves toward the gambling house, looks up, sees him, and becomes enraged*)

EUGENIO Signora maschera, alla sua salute. (*col bicchiere di vino fuor della finestra, fa un brindisi a Vittoria, non conoscendola*)

VITTORIA (*freme e dimena il capo*)

EUGENIO Comanda restar servita? È padrona, qui siamo tutti galantuomini. (*a Vittoria, come sopra*)

LISAURA Chi è questa maschera, che volete invitare? (*dalla finestra*)

VITTORIA (*smania*)

SCENA XXII

CAMERIERI *con altra portata vengono dalla locanda, ed entrano nella solita bottega, e detti*

RIDOLFO E chi paga? Il gonzo.

EUGENIO Signora maschera, se non vuol venire, non importa. Qui abbiamo qualche cosa meglio di lei. (*a Vittoria come sopra*)

VITTORIA Oimè! mi sento male. Non posso più.

RIDOLFO Signora maschera, si sente male? (*a Vittoria*)

VITTORIA Ah Ridolfo, aiutatemi per carità. (*si leva la maschera*)

RIDOLFO Ella è qui?

VITTORIA Son io pur troppo.

RIDOLFO Beva un poco di rosolio.

VITTORIA No, datemi dell'acqua.

RIDOLFO Eh, no acqua, vuol esser rosolio. Quando gli spirti sono oppressi, vi vuol qualche cosa che gli metta in moto. Favorisca, venga dentro.

VITTORIA Voglio andar su da quel cane; voglio ammazzarmi sugli occhi suoi.

RIDOLFO Per amor del cielo, venga qui, s'acquieti.

EUGENIO E viva quella bella giovanotta. Cari quegli occhi! (*bevendo*)

VITTORIA Lo sentite il briccone? Lo sentite? Lasciatemi andare.

RIDOLFO Non sarà mai vero, che io la lasci precipitare. (*la trattiene*)

EUGENIO (*with a glass of wine at the window, makes a toast to Vittoria, not recognizing her*) Masked lady, here's to your health.

VITTORIA (*trembles with rage and shakes her head*)

EUGENIO (*to Vittoria*) Would you like to join us? My lady, we are all gentlemen here.

LISAURA (*from the window*) Who is this mask that you want to invite?

VITTORIA (*more and more agitated*)

SCENE XXII

WAITERS *arrive from the inn with more food and enter the gambling house*

RIDOLFO And who's paying? The simpleton.

EUGENIO (*to Vittoria*) Masked lady, if you don't want to come up, it doesn't matter. We've something better than you here.

VITTORIA Oh my! I feel sick. I can't take it anymore.

RIDOLFO (*to Vittoria*) Masked lady, do you feel unwell?

VITTORIA Ah, Ridolfo, help me for pity's sake.
(*takes off the mask*)

RIDOLFO You? Here?

VITTORIA It's me, unfortunately.

RIDOLFO Have a little rosolio.

VITTORIA No, give me some water.

RIDOLFO No, not water. It has to be rosolio. When your spirits are down, you need something to lift them. Please, come inside.

VITTORIA I want to go up there where that dog is. I want to kill myself in front of his very eyes.

RIDOLFO For Heaven's sake, come here. Be calm.

EUGENIO (*drinking*) Here's to the lovely lass and her lovely eyes!

VITTORIA Do you hear the rogue? Do you hear him? Let me go.

RIDOLFO (*holding her back*) I would never let you do such a rash thing.

VITTORIA Non posso più. Aiuto, ch'io muoro.
(*cade svenuta*)
RIDOLFO Ora sto bene.
(*la va aiutando e sostenendo alla meglio*)

SCENA XXIII

PLACIDA *sulla porta della locanda, e detti*

PLACIDA Oh cielo! Dalla finestra mi parve sentire la voce di
mio marito; se fosse qui, sarei giunta bene in tempo a
svergognarlo. (*esce il cameriere dalla biscaccia*) Quel
giovine, ditemi in grazia, chi vi è lassù in quei camerini?
(*al cameriere che viene dalla biscaccia*)
CAMERIERE Tre galantuomini. Uno il signor Eugenio, l'altro
il signor Don Marzio, napoletano, ed il terzo il signor
conte Leandro Ardenti.
PLACIDA (Fra questi non vi è Flamminio, quando non si fosse
cangiato nome).
LEANDRO E viva la bella fortuna del signor Eugenio.
(*bevendo*)
TUTTI E viva.
PLACIDA (Questi è mio marito senz'altro). Caro galantuomo,
fatemi un piacere, conducetemi su da questi signori, che
voglio loro fare una burla. (*al cameriere*)
CAMERIERE Sarà servita. (Solita carica dei camerieri).
(*l'introduce per la solita bottega del giuoco*)
RIDOLFO Animo, prenda coraggio, non sarà niente.
(*a Vittoria*)
VITTORIA Io mi sento morire. (*rinviene*)
(*Dalle finestre dei camerini si vedono alzarsi tutti da tavola
in confusione per la sorpresa di Leandro vedendo Placida, e
perché mostra di volerla uccidere*)
EUGENIO No, fermatevi.
DON MARZIO Non fate.
LEANDRO Levati di qui.

VITTORIA I can't take it. Help me. I'm dying.
  (*faints*)
RIDOLFO Now, that's all I need.
  (*holds her up as best he can*)

SCENE XXIII

Enter PLACIDA *at the door of the inn*

PLACIDA Good Heavens! I thought I heard my husband's voice
  from the window. If he's here, I've come at the right
  moment to shame him.
  (*enter waiter from the gambling house*)
PLACIDA (*to waiter*) Young man, please tell me. Who's up there
  in those rooms?
WAITER Three gentlemen. One is Signor Eugenio, the other
  Signor Don Marzio from Naples, and the third is Count
  Leandro Ardenti.
PLACIDA (*aside*) Flaminio isn't among them, unless he changed
  his name.
LEANDRO (*drinking*) Here's to Eugenio's good fortune.
ALL Hurrah!
PLACIDA (*aside*) That's my husband for sure. (*to waiter*) Dear
  sir, do me a favor. Take me up to these gentlemen. I'd like
  to play a trick on them.
WAITER Right away, my lady. (*aside*) That's what waiters are for.
  (*he leads her into the gambling house*)
RIDOLFO (*to Vittoria*) Come now, be brave. It's nothing serious.
VITTORIA (*wakes up*) I feel I'm dying.
LEANDRO (*looks surprised when he sees Placida and acts like he's
  going to kill her. Through the windows all can be seen getting
  up from the table in confusion*)
EUGENIO No, stop!
DON MARZIO Don't do it.
LEANDRO Get out of here!
PLACIDA Help, help!

PLACIDA Aiuto, aiuto. (*fugge via per la scala, Leandro vuol seguitarla colla spada, Eugenio lo trattiene*)

TRAPPOLA (*con un tondino di roba in un tovagliuolo salta da una finestra, e fugge in bottega del caffè*)

PLACIDA (*esce dalla bisca correndo e fugge nella locanda*)

EUGENIO (*con arme alla mano in difesa di Placida, contro Leandro che la inseguisce*)

DON MARZIO (*esce pian piano dalla biscaccia, e fugge via dicendo*) Rumores fuge.

I CAMERIERI (*dalla bisca passano nella locanda e serrano la porta*)

VITTORIA (*resta in bottega, assistita da Ridolfo*)

LEANDRO Liberate il passo. Voglio entrare in quella locanda. (*colla spada alla mano contro Eugenio*)

EUGENIO No, non sarà mai vero. Siete un barbaro contro la vostra moglie, ed io la difenderò sino all'ultimo sangue.

LEANDRO Giuro al cielo, ve ne pentirete. (*incalza Eugenio colla spada*)

EUGENIO Non ho paura di voi. (*incalza Leandro e l'obbliga rinculare tanto, che trovando la casa della ballerina aperta, entra in quella, e si salva*)

SCENA XXIV

EUGENIO, VITTORIA *e* RIDOLFO

EUGENIO Vile, codardo, fuggi? Ti nascondi? Vien fuori, se hai coraggio. (*bravando verso la porta della ballerina*)

VITTORIA Se volete sangue, spargete il mio. (*si presenta ad Eugenio*)

EUGENIO Andate via di qui, donna pazza, donna senza cervello.

VITTORIA Non sarà mai vero ch'io mi stacchi viva da voi.

EUGENIO Corpo di bacco, andate via, che farò qualche sproposito. (*minacciandola colla spada*)

PLACIDA *(flees down the stairs; leandro tries to follow her with his sword; Eugenio holds him back; Trappola with a plate of food wrapped in a napkin jumps out of a window and runs into the coffee house; placida exits the gambling house and runs into the inn; Eugenio, with weapon in hand, defends Placida against Leandro who's following her)*

DON MARZIO *(exits quietly from the gambling house and flees)*
Rumores fuge.

WAITERS *(pass from the gambling house to the inn and close the door)*

VITTORIA *(remains in the coffee house with Ridolfo)*

LEANDRO *(with sword in hand, against Eugenio)* Make way. I want to enter the inn.

EUGENIO No, it shall never be. You've been terrible to your wife, and I will defend her to the death.

LEANDRO In the name of Heaven, you'll regret this. *(pressing Eugenio with his sword)*

EUGENIO I'm not afraid of you. *(advances on Leandro and forces him to draw back, so much so that when he finds the dancer's door open, he enters and saves himself)*

SCENE XXIV

EUGENIO *(toward the dancer's door)* You vile coward, why do you flee? Why do you hide? Come out, if you dare.

VITTORIA *(approaches Eugenio)* If you want blood, then shed mine.

EUGENIO Get out of here, you stupid, crazy woman.

VITTORIA As long as I live, I will never leave your side.

EUGENIO *(threatening her with his sword)* Confound you, get out of my way before I lose my temper.

RIDOLFO (*con arme alla mano corre in difesa di Vittoria, e si presenta contro Eugenio*) Che pretende di fare, padron mio? Che pretende? Crede per aver quella spada di atterrir tutto il mondo? Questa povera donna innocente, non ha nessuno, che la difenda, ma finché avrò sangue la difenderò io. Anche minacciarla? Dopo tanti strapazzi che le ha fatti, anche minacciarla? Signora venga con me e non abbia timor di niente. (*a Vittoria*)

VITTORIA No, caro Ridolfo; se mio marito vuol la mia morte, lasciate che si sodisfaccia. Via, ammazzami cane, assassino, traditore; ammazzami, disgraziato; uomo senza riputazione, senza cuore, senza coscienza.

EUGENIO (*rimette la spada nel fodero senza parlare, mortificato*)

RIDOLFO Ah, signor Eugenio, vedo che già è pentito, ed io le domando perdono, se troppo temerariamente ho parlato. V.S. sa se le voglio bene, e sa cosa ho fatto per lei, onde anche questo mio trasporto lo prenda per un effetto d'amore. Questa povera signora mi fa pietà. È possibile che le sue lagrime non inteneriscano il di lei cuore? (*ad Eugenio*)

EUGENIO (*si asciuga gli occhi, e non parla*)

RIDOLFO Osservi, signora Vittoria, osservi il signor Eugenio. (*piano a Vittoria*) Piange, è intenerito, si pentirà, muterà vita, stia sicura, che le vorrà bene.

VITTORIA Lagrime di coccodrillo. Quante volte mi ha promesso di mutar vita! Quante volte colle lagrime agli occhi mi ha incantata! Non gli credo più; è un traditore, non gli credo più.

EUGENIO (*freme tra il rossore e la rabbia. Getta il cappello in terra da disperato, e senza parlare va nella bottega interna del caffè*)

RIDOLFO (*runs to Vittoria's defense with weapon in hand and challenges Eugenio*) What do you think you're doing, Master? What are you doing? Do you think you can terrorize the world because of that sword? This poor, innocent woman may not have anyone to defend her, but I'll defend her to the death. How dare you threaten her, after the way you've treated her? How dare you? (*to Vittoria*) Signora, come with me and fear nothing.

VITTORIA No, dear Ridolfo. If my husband wants me dead, let him have his satisfaction. So then, kill me, you dog, assassin, traitor. Kill me, you scoundrel. You have neither honor, heart, nor conscience.

EUGENIO (*mortified, puts the sword back into its sheath without a word*)

RIDOLFO (*to Eugenio*) Ah, Signor Eugenio, I see that you are sorry, and I beg your pardon if I spoke too harshly. My lord, you know that I love you, and you know what I've done for you. Even this outburst of mine was the effect of love. I pity this poor woman. How can it be that her tears do not touch your heart?

EUGENIO dries his eyes and doesn't speak

RIDOLFO (*quietly to Vittoria*) Look, Signora Vittoria, look at Signor Eugenio. He's crying. He's calmed down. He will repent and mend his ways. Rest assured that he loves you.

VITTORIA Crocodile tears. How many times has he promised me that he would mend his ways? How many times has he fooled me with his tears? I won't believe him anymore. He's a traitor. I won't believe him anymore.

EUGENIO (*trembles, visibly moved and shaken; he throws his hat on the ground like a desperate man, and without a word he enters the back room of the coffee house*)

SCENA XXV

VITTORIA *e* RIDOLFO

VITTORIA Che vuol dire, che non parla? (*a Ridolfo*)

RIDOLFO È confuso.

VITTORIA Che si sia in un momento cambiato?

RIDOLFO Credo di sì. Le dirò; se tanto ella, che io, non facevamo altro che piangere e che pregare, si sarebbe sempre più imbestialito. Quel poco di muso duro che abbiamo fatto, quel poco di bravata, l'ha messo in soggezione, e l'ha fatto cambiare. Conosce il fallo, vorrebbe scusarsi, e non sa come fare.

VITTORIA Caro Ridolfo, andiamolo a consolare.

RIDOLFO Questa è una cosa che l'ha da fare V.S. senza di me.

VITTORIA Andate prima voi, sappiatemi dire come ho da contenermi.

RIDOLFO Volentieri. Vado a vedere; ma lo spero pentito. (*entra in bottega*)

SCENA XXVI

VITTORIA, *poi* RIDOLFO

VITTORIA Questa è l'ultima volta che mi vede piangere. O si pente, e sarà il mio caro marito; o persiste, e non sarò più buona a soffrirlo.

RIDOLFO Signora Vittoria, cattive nuove; non vi è più! È andato via per la porticina.

VITTORIA Non ve l'ho detto ch'è perfido, ch'è ostinato?

RIDOLFO Ed io credo che sia andato via per vergogna, pieno di confusione, per non aver coraggio di chiederle scusa, di domandarle perdono.

VITTORIA Eh che da una moglie tenera, come son io, sa egli quanto facilmente può ottenere il perdono.

SCENE XXV

VITTORIA What's the meaning of this silence?

RIDOLFO He's confused.

VITTORIA How can he have changed in one minute?

RIDOLFO I believe he has. Let me tell you something: if
both of us had done nothing but cry and beg, he
would have become more enraged. But we were a little
hardheaded, and we did some swaggering, and this
embarrassed him, and it made him change. He
recognizes his mistake, and now he'd like to be
forgiven, but he doesn't know how.

VITTORIA Dear Ridolfo, let's go and console him.

RIDOLFO That's something your ladyship must do without me.

VITTORIA You go first, and find out how I should behave.

RIDOLFO Gladly. I'll go and see, but I expect to find that he's
repented. (*enters the shop*)

SCENE XXVI

VITTORIA This is the last time that he'll see me cry. Either he'll
repent, and he'll be my dear husband again, or he'll keep this
up, and I won't be able to bear it any longer. (*enter Ridolfo*)

RIDOLFO Signora Vittoria, bad news. He's not here anymore!
He left through the backdoor.

VITTORIA Didn't I tell you that he's treacherous, that he's stubborn?

RIDOLFO I believe that he left out of shame. He's confused
since he didn't have the courage to say he's sorry and ask for
your forgiveness.

VITTORIA Yes, he knows how easy it is to be forgiven by a
loving wife like me.

RIDOLFO Osservi. È andato via senza il cappello.
(*prende il cappello in terra*)
VITTORIA Perché è un pazzo.
RIDOLFO Perché è confuso; non sa quel che si faccia.
VITTORIA Ma se è pentito, perché non dirmelo?
RIDOLFO Non ha coraggio.
VITTORIA Ridolfo, voi mi lusingate.
RIDOLFO Faccia così: si ritiri nel mio camerino; lasci che
io vada a ritrovarlo, e spero di condurglielo qui, come
un cagnuolino.
VITTORIA Quanto sarebbe meglio, che non ci pensassi più!
RIDOLFO Anche per questa volta faccia a modo mio, e spero
non si pentirà.
VITTORIA Sì, così farò. Vi aspetterò nel camerino. Voglio poter
dire, che ho fatto tutto per un marito. Ma se egli se ne
abusa, giuro di cambiare in altrettanto sdegno l'amore.
(*entra nella bottega interna*)
RIDOLFO Se fosse un mio figlio, non avrei tanta pena.
(*parte*)

SCENA XXVII

LISAURA *sola dalla bottega del giuoco, osservando se vi è nessuno
che la veda*

Oh! povera me, che paura! Ah conte briccone! Ha moglie, e
mi lusinga di volermi sposare! In casa mia non lo voglio
mai più. Quant'era meglio ch'io seguitassi a ballare e non
concepissi la malinconia di diventare contessa. Piace un
poco troppo a noi altre donne il viver senza fatica. (*entra
nella sua casa e chiude la porta*)

RIDOLFO Look. He left without his hat.
  (*picks up the hat*)
VITTORIA Because he's crazy.
RIDOLFO Because he's confused. He doesn't know what
  he's doing.
VITTORIA But if he's sorry, why doesn't he say so?
RIDOLFO He doesn't have the courage.
VITTORIA Ridolfo, I almost want to believe you.
RIDOLFO Do this: go to the back room. Let me go find him,
  and hopefully I'll bring him back here like a little puppy.
VITTORIA It would be much better for me to forget about him!
RIDOLFO Do what I say one more time, and you won't regret it.
VITTORIA Yes, I'll do what you say. I'll wait for you in the
  back room. I'd like to be able to say that I've done
  everything I can for my husband. But if he takes
  advantage of me, I swear that my love will surely
  turn to scorn. (*enters the back of the shop*)
RIDOLFO I couldn't feel more sorry for him if he were my own
  son. (*exit Ridolfo*)

SCENE XXVII

Enter LISAURA *alone from the gambling house looking around to
make sure no one sees her*

LISAURA Oh! Woe is me! How awful! Ah, the Count is a rogue!
  He already has a wife, and he claims he wants to marry
  me! I don't want him in my house. I should have kept
  on dancing instead of dreaming that I could become
  a countess. We women are a little overfond of living
  without working. (*enters her house and closes the door*)

ATTO TERZO

SCENA I

LEANDRO, *scacciato di casa da* LISAURA

LEANDRO A me un simile trattamento?
LISAURA (*sulla porta*) Sì, a voi, falsario, impostore.
LEANDRO Di che vi potete dolere di me? D'aver abbandonata
mia moglie per causa vostra?
LISAURA Se avessi saputo ch'eravate ammogliato, non vi avrei
ricevuto in mia casa.
LEANDRO Non sono stato io il primo a venirvi.
LISAURA Siete però stato l'ultimo.

SCENA II

DON MARZIO, *che osserva coll'occhialetto e ride fra sé, e detti*

LEANDRO Non avete meco gittato il tempo.
LISAURA Sì, sono stata anch'io a parte de' vostri indegni
profitti. Arrossisco in pensarlo; andate al diavolo, e non vi
accostate più a questa casa.
LEANDRO Ci verrò a prendere la mia roba.
DON MARZIO (*ride e burla di nascosto Leandro*)
LISAURA La vostra roba vi sarà consegnata dalla mia serva.
(*entra e chiude la porta*)
LEANDRO A me un insulto di questa sorta? Me la pagherai.
DON MARZIO (*ride, e voltandosi Leandro, si compone in
serietà*)
LEANDRO Amico, avete veduto?
DON MARZIO Che cosa? Vengo in questo punto.

ACT THREE

SCENE I

Enter LEANDRO, *kicked out of* LISAURA'S *house*

LEANDRO How dare you treat me so?
LISAURA (*at the door*) Because you're a liar, an impostor.
LEANDRO What have I ever done wrong to you? Do you call abandoning my wife for you something wrong?
LISAURA If I had known you were married, I wouldn't have ever received you in my home.
LEANDRO I wasn't the first to come here.
LISAURA But you'll be the last.

SCENE II

Enter DON MARZIO *looking on with his lorgnette and laughing to himself*

LEANDRO You didn't waste your time with me.
LISAURA Yes, I too enjoyed your tawdry profits. I'm ashamed just to think of it. Go to hell and don't come around here anymore.
LEANDRO I'll come by to collect my things.
DON MARZIO (*laughs and makes fun of Leandro behind his back*)
LISAURA My servant will bring you your things. (*enters the house and closes the door*)
LEANDRO How dare you insult me so? You'll pay for this.
DON MARZIO (*laughs, and when Leandro turns around, assumes a serious air*)
LEANDRO Friend, did you see that?
DON MARZIO See what? I just got here.

LEANDRO Non avete veduto la ballerina sulla porta?

DON MARZIO No certamente, non l'ho veduta.

LEANDRO (Manco male). (*da sé*)

DON MARZIO Venite qua; parlatemi da galantuomo,
confidatevi con me, e state sicuro che i fatti vostri
non si sapranno da chi che sia. Voi siete forestiere,
come sono io, ma io ho più pratica del paese di voi.
Se vi occorre protezione, assistenza, consiglio,
e sopratutto segretezza, son qua io. Fate capitale di me.
Di cuore, con premura, da buon amico; senza che
nessun sappia niente.

LEANDRO Giacché con tanta bontà vi esibite di favorirmi,
aprirò a voi tutto il mio cuore, ma per amor del cielo vi
raccomando la segretezza.

DON MARZIO Andiamo avanti.

LEANDRO Sappiate che la pellegrina è mia moglie.

DON MARZIO Buono!

LEANDRO Che l'ho abbandonata in Torino.

DON MARZIO (Oh che briccone!) (*da sé, guardandolo con
l'occhialetto*)

LEANDRO Sappiate ch'io non sono altrimenti il conte
Leandro.

DON MARZIO (Meglio!) (*da sé, come sopra*)

LEANDRO I miei natali non sono nobili.

DON MARZIO Non sareste già figliuolo di qualche birro?

LEANDRO Mi maraviglio, signore, son nato povero, ma di
gente onorata.

DON MARZIO Via, via: tirate avanti.

LEANDRO Il mio esercizio era di scritturale . . .

DON MARZIO Troppa fatica non è egli vero?

LEANDRO E desiderando vedere il mondo . . .

DON MARZIO Alle spalle de' gonzi.

LEANDRO Son venuto a Venezia . . .

DON MARZIO A far il birbante.

LEANDRO Ma voi mi strapazzate. Questa non è la maniera
di trattare.

LEANDRO You didn't see the dancer at the door?

DON MARZIO I certainly did not.

LEANDRO (*aside*) Thank God.

DON MARZIO Come here. Speak to me as a true gentleman. Confide in me and rest assured that no one whosoever will find out about your affairs. You're a stranger, as I am, but I've been around here longer than you. Should you need protection, assistance, advice, and above all secrecy, you can count on me. You can trust me. From the heart: a caring and good friend. No one will ever find out anything.

LEANDRO Since you show such goodness toward me, I will open my heart to you. But for Heaven's sake, secrecy is of utmost importance.

DON MARZIO Go on.

LEANDRO I want you to know that the wayfarer is my wife.

DON MARZIO Good Lord!

LEANDRO The wife I abandoned in Turin.

DON MARZIO (*aside, looking at him through his lorgnette*) Oh, what a rogue!

LEANDRO Besides this, I'll have you know that I am not Count Leandro.

DON MARZIO (*aside*) Better yet!

LEANDRO I was not born of noble blood.

DON MARZIO You wouldn't happen to be the son of a dirty policeman, would you?

LEANDRO You surprise me, sir. I was born poor, but to respectable people nonetheless.

DON MARZIO Yes, yes. Go on.

LEANDRO I was a clerk. . . .

DON MARZIO Hard work, eh?

LEANDRO And since I wanted to see the world . . .

DON MARZIO At the expense of simpletons.

LEANDRO I came to Venice.

DON MARZIO To be a knave.

LEANDRO You're being too rough on me. That's no way to treat a friend.

DON MARZIO Sentite; io ho promesso proteggervi, e lo farò;
ho promesso segretezza, e la osserverò; ma fra voi e
me avete da permettermi che possa dirvi qualche
cosa amorosamente.

LEANDRO Vedete il caso in cui mi ritrovo; se mia moglie mi
scopre, sono esposto a qualche disgrazia.

DON MARZIO Che pensereste di fare?

LEANDRO Si potrebbe vedere di far cacciar via di Venezia colei.

DON MARZIO Via, via. Si vede che siete un briccone.

LEANDRO Come parlate, signore?

DON MARZIO Fra voi e me, amorosamente.

LEANDRO Dunque anderò via io; basta che colei non
lo sappia.

DON MARZIO Da me, non lo saprà certamente.

LEANDRO Mi consigliate ch'io parta?

DON MARZIO Sì, questo è il miglior ripiego. Andate subito.
Prendete una gondola; fatevi condurre a Fusina, prendete
le poste e andatevene a Ferrara.

LEANDRO Anderò questa sera; già poco manca alla notte.
Voglio prima levar le mie poche robe, che sono qui in
casa della ballerina.

DON MARZIO Fate presto e andate via subito. Non vi fate
vedere.

LEANDRO Uscirò per la porta di dietro, per non essere veduto.

DON MARZIO (Lo diceva io; si serve per la porta di dietro).
(*da sé*)

LEANDRO Sopra tutto vi raccomando la segretezza.

DON MARZIO Di questa siete sicuro.

LEANDRO Vi prego d'una grazia; datele questi due zecchini;
poi mandatela via. Scrivetemi, e torno subito.
(*gli dà due zecchini*)

DON MARZIO Le darò i due zecchini. Andate via.

LEANDRO Ma assicuratevi che ella parta . . .

DON MARZIO Andate, che siate maladetto.

LEANDRO Mi scacciate?

DON MARZIO Ve lo dico amorosamente, per vostro bene; andate
che il diavolo vi porti.

DON MARZIO Listen, I promised to protect you, and I will.
I promised you secrecy and that you will have. This is
between you and me, but you must allow me to tell
you—from the heart—what I think.
LEANDRO You see my predicament. If my wife finds me out,
I'll be in a lot of trouble.
DON MARZIO What do you think you'll do?
LEANDRO We could try to have her chased out of Venice.
DON MARZIO Oh, come, come. It's obvious that you're
a rogue.
LEANDRO Sir, how you speak!
DON MARZIO Between you and me, from the heart.
LEANDRO Then I'll be the one to leave. The important thing
is that she not learn of it.
DON MARZIO She certainly won't find out from me.
LEANDRO Is your advice that I leave?
DON MARZIO Yes, this is the best remedy. Leave right away.
Take a gondola. Have them take you to Fusina. Take the
coach to Ferrara.
LEANDRO I'll leave tonight. It's almost dark. I want first
to get what little things I have here at the dancer's
house.
DON MARZIO Hurry and leave right away. Don't let yourself
be seen.
LEANDRO I'll leave by the back door so as not to be seen.
DON MARZIO (*aside*) I knew it. He uses the backdoor.
LEANDRO Above all I implore you to keep it a secret.
DON MARZIO You can be sure of that.
LEANDRO I beg you to do me a favor: give her these two
sequins. Then send her away. Write me, and I'll return
right away. (*gives him two sequins*)
DON MARZIO I'll give her the two sequins. Leave.
LEANDRO But make sure that she leaves. . . .
DON MARZIO Leave, damn you.
LEANDRO Are you chasing me away?
DON MARZIO I'm telling you, from the heart, for your own
good: get the devil out of here.

LEANDRO (Oh, che razza di uomo! Se strapazza gli amici,
che farà poi coi nemici!)
(*va in casa di Lisaura*)
DON MARZIO Il signor conte! Briccone! Il signor conte! Se
non si fosse raccomandato a me, gli farei romper l'ossa
di bastonate.

SCENA III

PLACIDA *dalla locanda, e detto*

PLACIDA Sì, nasca quel che può nascere, voglio ritrovare
quell'indegno di mio marito.
DON MARZIO Pellegrina, come va?
PLACIDA Voi, se non m'inganno, siete uno di quelli che
erano alla tavola con mio marito.
DON MARZIO Sì, son quello delle castagne secche.
PLACIDA Per carità, ditemi dove si trova quel traditore.
DON MARZIO Io non lo so, e quando anco lo sapessi,
non ve lo direi.
PLACIDA Per che causa?
DON MARZIO Perché, se lo trovate, farete peggio. Vi
ammazzerà.
PLACIDA Pazienza. Avrò terminato almen di penare.
DON MARZIO Eh spropositi! Bestialità! Ritornate
a Torino.
PLACIDA Senza mio marito?
DON MARZIO Sì, senza vostro marito. Ormai, che volete
fare? È un briccone.
PLACIDA Pazienza! Almeno vorrei vederlo.
DON MARZIO Oh non lo vedete più.
PLACIDA Per carità, ditemi, se lo sapete; è egli forse
partito?
DON MARZIO È partito, e non è partito.
PLACIDA Per quel che vedo, V.S. sa qualche cosa di
mio marito.

LEANDRO (*aside*) What kind of man is he? If he's this rough with his friends, I wonder how he treats his enemies! (*enters Lisaura's house*)

DON MARZIO Signor Count! What a rogue! Signor Count! If he hadn't sought my protection, I'd have his bones broken with a cudgel.

SCENE III

Enter PLACIDA *from the inn*

PLACIDA Yes, come what may, I want to find that no-good husband of mine.

DON MARZIO Wayfarer, how's it going?

PLACIDA If I'm not mistaken, you were among those who dined with my husband.

DON MARZIO Yes, I'm the one with the dried chestnuts.

PLACIDA I beg you, tell me where I can find that traitor.

DON MARZIO I don't know. And even if I did, I wouldn't tell you.

PLACIDA For what reason?

DON MARZIO Because you're better off not finding him. He'll murder you.

PLACIDA That doesn't matter! At least my suffering will have ended.

DON MARZIO What nonsense! That's sheer idiocy! Go back to Turin.

PLACIDA Without my husband?

DON MARZIO Yes, without your husband. What's left for you to do now? He's a rogue.

PLACIDA That doesn't matter! I'd like to see him at least.

DON MARZIO Oh, you won't see him anymore.

PLACIDA Please tell me, if you know. Could it be that he's left?

DON MARZIO He did, and he didn't.

PLACIDA It seems to me, my lord, that you know something about my husband.

DON MARZIO Io? So, e non so, ma non parlo.

PLACIDA Signore, movetevi a compassione di me.

DON MARZIO Andate a Torino, e non pensate ad altro. Tenete, vi dono questi due zecchini.

PLACIDA Il cielo vi rimeriti la vostra carità; ma non volete dirmi nulla di mio marito? Pazienza! Me ne anderò disperata. (*in atto di partire piangendo*)

DON MARZIO (Povera donna!) (*da sé*) Ehi. (*la chiama*)

PLACIDA Signore.

DON MARZIO Vostro marito è qui in casa della ballerina, che prende la sua roba, e partirà per la porta di dietro. (*parte*)

PLACIDA È in Venezia! Non è partito! È in casa della ballerina! Se avessi qualcheduno che mi assistesse, vorrei di bel nuovo azzardarmi. Ma così sola, temo di qualche insulto.

SCENA IV

RIDOLFO *ed* EUGENIO, *e detta*

RIDOLFO Eh via, cosa sono queste difficoltà? Siamo tutti uomini, tutti soggetti ad errare. Quando l'uomo si pente, la virtù del pentimento cancella tutto il demerito dei mancamenti.

EUGENIO Tutto va bene, ma mia moglie non mi crederà più.

RIDOLFO Venga con me; lasci parlare a me. La signora Vittoria le vuol bene; tutto si aggiusterà.

PLACIDA Signor Eugenio.

RIDOLFO Il signor Eugenio si contenti di lasciarlo stare. Ha altro che fare, che badare a lei.

PLACIDA Io non pretendo di sviarlo da' suoi interessi. Mi raccomando a tutti, nello stato miserabile in cui mi ritrovo.

DON MARZIO Who? Me? I know, and I don't know. But I
   don't gossip.
PLACIDA Sir, have pity on me.
DON MARZIO Go back to Turin and forget about it. Here,
   I'll give you two sequins.
PLACIDA Bless you for your kindness. But won't you want to
   tell me about my husband? So be it! (*starts to leave crying*)
   I'll leave. It's hopeless.
DON MARZIO (*aside*) Poor woman! (*calling Placida*) I say!
PLACIDA Sir.
DON MARZIO Your husband is here in the dancer's house
   getting his things, and he'll leave through the back door.
   (*exit Don Marzio*)
PLACIDA He's in Venice! He hasn't left! He's in the dancer's
   house! If I could find someone to help me, I'd like to
   hazard it again. But all alone, I'm afraid I'll get nothing
   but insults.

SCENE IV

Enter RIDOLFO *and* EUGENIO

RIDOLFO Oh, come on, what's so difficult about that. We're
   all human, all liable to make mistakes. When a man
   repents, the goodness of his repentance cancels the
   shame of his shortcomings.
EUGENIO That's all very good, but my wife wouldn't believe
   me anymore.
RIDOLFO Come with me. Leave the talking to me. Signora
   Vittoria loves you. Everything will work out.
PLACIDA Signor Eugenio.
RIDOLFO Be good enough to leave Signor Eugenio in peace.
   He has other things to do besides taking care of you.
PLACIDA I don't expect him to neglect his affairs for me. I'm
   begging both of you to help me out of the miserable
   state in which I find myself.

EUGENIO Credetemi, Ridolfo, che questa povera donna merita compassione; è onestissima, e suo marito è un briccone.

PLACIDA Egli mi ha abbandonata in Torino. Lo ritrovo in Venezia, tenta uccidermi, ed ora è sulle mosse per fuggirmi nuovamente di mano.

RIDOLFO Sa ella dove egli sia?

PLACIDA È qui in casa della ballerina; mette insieme le sue robe, e fra poco se n'andrà.

RIDOLFO Se andrà via, lo vedrà.

PLACIDA Partirà per la porta di dietro, ed io non lo vedrò, o se sarò scoperta, mi ucciderà.

RIDOLFO Chi ha detto che anderà via per la porta di dietro?

PLACIDA Quel signore che si chiama Don Marzio.

RIDOLFO La tromba della comunità. Faccia così; si ritiri in bottega qui del barbiere; stando lì, si vede la porticina segreta. Subito che lo vede uscire, mi avvisi, e lasci operare a me.

PLACIDA In quella bottega non mi vorranno.

RIDOLFO Ora. Ehi, messer Agabito? (*chiama*)

SCENA V

Il GARZONE *del barbiere dalla sua bottega, e detti*

GARZONE Che volete messer Ridolfo?

RIDOLFO Dite al vostro padrone che mi faccia il piacere di tener questa pellegrina in bottega per un poco, fino che venga io a ripigliarla.

GARZONE Volentieri. Venga, venga padrona, che imparerà a fare la barba. Benché per pelare, la ne saprà più di noi altri barbieri. (*rientra in bottega*)

PLACIDA Tutto mi convien soffrire per causa di quell'indegno. Povere donne! È meglio affogarsi, che maritarsi così. (*entra dal barbiere*)

EUGENIO Believe me, Ridolfo, this poor woman deserves
sympathy. She's most honest, and her husband's a rogue.
PLACIDA He abandoned me in Turin. I find him in Venice. He
tries to kill me. And now he's planning to slip through my
hands once again.
RIDOLFO Do you know where he is?
PLACIDA He's here at the dancer's house getting his things
together, and he'll be leaving before long.
RIDOLFO When he leaves, you'll see him.
PLACIDA He'll leave through the back door, and I won't see
him. And if he discovers me, he'll kill me.
RIDOLFO Who said that he'll leave through the backdoor?
PLACIDA That gentleman named Don Marzio.
RIDOLFO The town-crier. Do this: go inside the barbershop.
From there you can see the secret door. As soon as
you see him leave, tell me and leave the rest to me.
PLACIDA They may not want me in that shop.
RIDOLFO Now they will. (*calling*) Master Agabito?

SCENE V

Enter the barber's boy from the barbershop

BOY What do you want, Master Ridolfo?
RIDOLFO Tell your master to take in this wayfarer for a
little while, until I come back to fetch her—as a favor
to me.
BOY Gladly. Come along, your ladyship. You'll learn how to
shave. Although, when it comes to fleecing, you could
probably teach us barbers something. (*reenters the shop*)
PLACIDA I have to suffer all this because of that scoundrel. Poor
women! We'd be better off drowning than landing a bad
husband. (*enters the barbershop*)

SCENA VI

RIDOLFO *ed* EUGENIO

RIDOLFO Se posso, voglio vedere di far del bene, anche a questa
povera diavola. E nello stesso tempo facendola partire con
suo marito, la signora Vittoria non avrà più di lei gelosia.
Già mi ha detto qualche cosa della pellegrina.

EUGENIO Voi siete un uomo di buon cuore. In caso di
bisogno troverete cento amici che s'impiegheranno
per voi.

RIDOLFO Prego il cielo di non aver bisogno di nessuno. In tal
caso non so che cosa potessi sperare. Al mondo vi è
dell'ingratitudine assai.

EUGENIO Di me potrete disporre, fin ch'io viva.

RIDOLFO La ringrazio infinitamente. Ma badiamo a noi.
Che pens'ella di fare? Vuol andar in camerino da sua
moglie, o vuol farla venire in bottega? Vuol andar solo?
Vuole che venga anch'io? Comandi.

EUGENIO In bottega non istà bene; se venite anche voi, avrà
soggezione. Se vado solo, mi vorrà cavare gli occhi . . .
Non importa; ch'ella si sfoghi, che poi la collera passerà.
Anderò solo.

RIDOLFO Vada pure col nome del cielo.

EUGENIO Se bisogna, vi chiamerò.

RIDOLFO Si ricordi, che io non servo per testimonio.

EUGENIO Oh, che caro Ridolfo! Vado.
      (*in atto d'incamminarsi*)

RIDOLFO Via, bravo.

EUGENIO Che cosa credete che abbia da essere?

RIDOLFO Bene.

EUGENIO Pianti, o graffiature?

RIDOLFO Un poco di tutto.

EUGENIO E poi?

RIDOLFO Ognun dal canto suo cura si prenda.

EUGENIO Se non chiamo, non venite.

RIDOLFO Già ci s'intende.

SCENE VI

RIDOLFO If I can, I'd like to try to help this poor wretch, too.
At the same time, if I get her to leave with her husband,
Signora Vittoria won't be jealous anymore. She's already
said something to me about the wayfarer.

EUGENIO You're a goodhearted man. In case of need, a hundred
friends will offer their service to you.

RIDOLFO I pray to Heaven that I won't need anyone. In such a
case, I wouldn't know what to expect. There's plenty of
ingratitude in the world.

EUGENIO You can count on me as long as I live.

RIDOLFO I'm eternally thankful. But let's get back to us. What
are you planning to do? Do you want to go in the back
room with your wife, or do you want her to come into the
shop? Do you want to go alone? Do you want me to come
too? Just give the word.

EUGENIO The coffee house won't do. If you come, she'll be
embarrassed. If I go alone she'll tear my eyes out. . . . It
doesn't matter. Let her get it off her chest. Her anger will
pass. I'll go alone.

RIDOLFO Go then, and may Heaven protect you.

EUGENIO If I need to, I'll call you.

RIDOLFO Remember. You don't need a witness.

EUGENIO (*about to leave*) Oh, you're quite a fellow, Ridolfo!
I'll go.

RIDOLFO Get on with it.

EUGENIO How do you think it will go?

RIDOLFO Well.

EUGENIO Crying or scratching?

RIDOLFO A little bit of everything.

EUGENIO And then?

RIDOLFO Every man for himself.

EUGENIO Don't come unless I call.

RIDOLFO Understood.

EUGENIO Vi racconterò tutto.

RIDOLFO Via, andate.

EUGENIO (Grand'uomo è Ridolfo! Gran buon amico!)
   (*entra nella bottega interna*)

SCENA VII

RIDOLFO, *poi* TRAPPOLA *e giovani*

RIDOLFO Marito e moglie? Gli lascio stare quanto vogliono.
   Ehi, Trappola, giovani, dove siete!

TRAPPOLA Son qui.

RIDOLFO Badate alla bottega, che io vado qui dal barbiere.
   Se il signor Eugenio mi vuole, chiamatemi, che vengo
   subito.

TRAPPOLA Posso andar io, a far compagnia al signor Eugenio?

RIDOLFO Signor no, non avete da andare, e badate bene che là
   dentro non vi vada nessuno.

TRAPPOLA Ma perché?

RIDOLFO Perché no.

TRAPPOLA Anderò a veder se vuol niente.

RIDOLFO Non andar, se non chiama. (Voglio intendere un po'
   meglio dalla pellegrina, come va questo suo negozio, e se
   posso, voglio vedere d'accomodarlo). (*entra dal barbiere*)

SCENA VIII

TRAPPOLA, *poi* DON MARZIO

TRAPPOLA Appunto, perché mi ha detto che non vi vada, son
   curioso d'andarvi.

DON MARZIO Trappola, hai avuto paura?

TRAPPOLA Un poco.

DON MARZIO Si è più veduto il signor Eugenio?

TRAPPOLA Sì signore, si è veduto; anzi è lì dentro. Ma! zitto.

EUGENIO I'll tell you everything.

RIDOLFO Go on, be on your way.

EUGENIO (*aside*) What a great man this Ridolfo! A great friend!
(*enters the back of the shop*)

SCENE VII

RIDOLFO Husband and wife? I'll let them be alone as long as
they need. Trappola, boys, where are you?
(*enter Trappola and boys*)

TRAPPOLA Here I am.

RIDOLFO Mind the shop. I'm going to the barber's. If Signor
Eugenio wants me, call me and I'll come right away.

TRAPPOLA May I go keep Signor Eugenio company?

RIDOLFO No sir. You mustn't go back there. And make sure
that no one goes back there.

TRAPPOLA But why not?

RIDOLFO Because I say so.

TRAPPOLA I'll go see if he needs anything.

RIDOLFO Don't go unless he calls. (*aside*) I want to hear more
from the wayfarer and see how her affairs are going . . . see
if I can be of assistance. (*enters the barbershop*)

SCENE VIII

TRAPPOLA I'm eager to go back there precisely because he told
me not to. (*enter Don Marzio*)

DON MARZIO Trappola, were you scared?

TRAPPOLA A little.

DON MARZIO Have you seen Signor Eugenio since?

TRAPPOLA Yes, sir, I've see him: he's back there. But . . . be quiet.

DON MARZIO Dove?

TRAPPOLA Zitto; nel camerino.

DON MARZIO Che vi fa? Giuoca?

TRAPPOLA Signor sì, giuoca. (*ridendo*)

DON MARZIO Con chi?

TRAPPOLA Con sua moglie. (*sotto voce*)

DON MARZIO Vi è sua moglie?

TRAPPOLA Vi è; ma zitto.

DON MARZIO Voglio andarlo a ritrovare.

TRAPPOLA Non si può.

DON MARZIO Perché?

TRAPPOLA Il padrone non vuole.

DON MARZIO Eh via, buffone. (*vuol andare*)

TRAPPOLA Le dico, che non si va.
   (*lo ferma*)

DON MARZIO Ti dico, che voglio andare. (*come sopra*)

TRAPPOLA Ed io dico, che non anderà. (*come sopra*)

DON MARZIO Ti caricherò di bastonate.

SCENA IX

RIDOLFO *dalla bottega del barbiere, e detti*

RIDOLFO Che c'è?

TRAPPOLA Vuol andar per forza a giuocar in terzo col matrimonio.

RIDOLFO Si contenti, signore, che là dentro non vi si va.

DON MARZIO Ed io ci voglio andare.

RIDOLFO In bottega mia comando io, e non vi anderà. Porti rispetto, se non vuol che ricorra. E voi, finché torno, là dentro non lasciate entrar chicchessia.
   (*a Trappola ed altri garzoni; poi batte alla casa della ballerina ed entra*)

DON MARZIO Where?

TRAPPOLA Be quiet. In the back room.

DON MARZIO What's he doing there? Is he gambling?

TRAPPOLA (*laughing*) Yes, sir, he's gambling.

DON MARZIO With whom?

TRAPPOLA (*whispering*) With his wife.

DON MARZIO Is his wife there?

TRAPPOLA She's there. But be quiet.

DON MARZIO I want to go see him.

TRAPPOLA You can't.

DON MARZIO Why not?

TRAPPOLA My master won't allow it.

DON MARZIO Get out of here, you buffoon. (*tries to go in*)

TRAPPOLA (*stopping him*) I'm telling you that you're not going back there.

DON MARZIO I'm telling you that I will.

TRAPPOLA And I'm telling you that you won't.

DON MARZIO I'll shower you with blows.

SCENE IX

Enter RIDOLFO *from the barbershop*

RIDOLFO What's going on?

TRAPPOLA He insists on playing the third wheel in the game of marriage.

RIDOLFO Content yourself, sir, that nobody is going there.

DON MARZIO But I insist on going there.

RIDOLFO In my shop, I'm in charge, and you won't be going back there. Have some respect, if you don't want me to resort to drastic measures. (*to Trappola and the boys*) And you, until I get back, don't let anyone go back there, no matter who. (*knocks on the dancer's door and enters*)

SCENA X

DON MARZIO, TRAPPOLA e GARZONI; *poi* PANDOLFO

TRAPPOLA Ha sentito? Al matrimonio si porta rispetto.

DON MARZIO (A un par mio? Non vi anderà? . . .
Porti rispetto? . . . A un par mio? E sto cheto?
E non parlo? E non lo bastono? Briccone!
Villanaccio! A me? A me?) (*da sé, sempre
passeggiando*) Caffè. (*siede*)

TRAPPOLA Subito. (*va a prendere il caffè e glielo porta*)

PANDOLFO Illustrissimo, ho bisogno della sua protezione.

DON MARZIO Che c'è, biscacciere?

PANDOLFO C'è del male.

DON MARZIO Che male c'è? Confidami, che t'aiuterò.

PANDOLFO Sappia, signore, che ci sono dei maligni
invidiosi, che non vorrebbero veder bene ai poveri
uomini. Vedono che io m'ingegno onoratamente
per mantenere con decoro la mia famiglia, e
questi bricconi mi hanno dato una querela di baro
di carte.

DON MARZIO Bricconi! Un galantuomo della tua sorta! Come
l'hai saputo? (*ironico*)

PANDOLFO Me l'ha detto un amico. Mi confido però che non
hanno prove, perché nella mia bottega praticano tutti
galantuomini, e niuno può dir male di me.

DON MARZIO Oh s'io avessi da esaminarmi contro di te, ne so
delle belle della tua abilità!

PANDOLFO Caro illustrissimo, per amor del cielo, la non mi
rovini; mi raccomando alla sua carità, alla sua protezione,
per le mie povere creature.

DON MARZIO Via, sì, t'assisterò, ti proteggerò. Lascia fare a me.
Ma bada bene. Carte segnate ne hai in bottega?

PANDOLFO Io non le segno . . . Ma qualche giuocatore si
diletta . . .

DON MARZIO Presto, abbruciale subito. Io non parlo.

PANDOLFO Ho paura non aver tempo per abbruciarle.

SCENE X

TRAPPOLA Did you hear that? Marriage is to be respected.

DON MARZIO (*aside, pacing*) To someone of my station? You won't be going . . . ? To someone of my station? Have some respect . . . ? And I remain silent? And I say nothing? And do I not beat him up? Scoundrel! Boorish upstart! To me? To me? (*to Trappola*) Coffee. (*sits down*)

TRAPPOLA Right away. (*goes to get him the coffee and brings it to him*) (*enter Pandolfo*)

PANDOLFO Your grace, I am in need of your protection.

DON MARZIO What's the matter, gambler?

PANDOLFO Something bad.

DON MARZIO What's wrong? Confide in me, and I'll help you.

PANDOLFO I'll have you know, sir, that there are some evil, envious people who don't like to see a poor man do well. These rogues see that I honestly strive to maintain my family with dignity, and they have charged me with cheating at cards.

DON MARZIO (*ironically*) What rogues! A gentleman like you! How did you find out?

PANDOLFO A friend told me. I trust, however, that they don't have proof because all those who frequent my gambling house are gentlemen, and no one can speak ill of me.

DON MARZIO Oh, if only I were called as witness, I know all about your finer abilities.

PANDOLFO Your grace, for Heaven's sake, don't ruin me. I appeal to your mercy for help, on account of my little ones.

DON MARZIO All right, yes, I'll help you. I'll protect you. Leave it to me. But be careful. Do you have any marked cards in there?

PANDOLFO I don't mark them . . . but some of the players may have indulged. . . .

DON MARZIO Hurry. Burn them right away. I won't talk.

PANDOLFO I'm afraid that I won't have time to burn them.

DON MARZIO Nascondile.

PANDOLFO Vado in bottega e le nascondo subito.

DON MARZIO Dove le vuoi nascondere?

PANDOLFO Ho un luogo segreto sotto le travature, che né anche il diavolo le ritrova. (*entra in bottega del giuoco*)

DON MARZIO Va, che sei un gran furbo!

SCENA XI

DON MARZIO, *poi un* CAPO DI BIRRI *mascherato ed altri birri nascosti, poi* TRAPPOLA

DON MARZIO Costui è alla vigilia della galera. Se trova alcuno che scopra la metà delle sue bricconate, lo pigliano prigione immediatamente.

CAPO (Girate qui d'intorno, e quando chiamo, venite) (*ai birri sulla cantonata della strada, i quali si ritirano*)

DON MARZIO (Carte segnate! Oh che ladri!) (*da sé*)

CAPO Caffè. (*siede*)

TRAPPOLA La servo. (*va per il caffè, e lo porta*)

CAPO Abbiamo delle belle giornate.

DON MARZIO Il tempo non vuol durare.

CAPO Pazienza. Godiamolo finché è buono.

DON MARZIO Lo godremo per poco.

CAPO Quando è mal tempo, si va in un casino e si giuoca.

DON MARZIO Basta andare in luoghi dove non rubino.

CAPO Qui, questa bottega vicina mi pare onorata.

DON MARZIO Onorata? È un ridotto di ladri.

CAPO Mi pare sia messer Pandolfo il padrone.

DON MARZIO Egli per l'appunto.

CAPO Per dir il vero, ho sentito dire che sia un giuocator di vantaggio.

DON MARZIO È un baro solennissimo.

DON MARZIO Hide them.

PANDOLFO I'll go to my shop and hide them right away.

DON MARZIO Where do you intend to hide them?

PANDOLFO I have a secret place under the rafters where the devil himself couldn't find them. (*enters the gambling house*)

DON MARZIO Go on, you crafty fellow!

SCENE XI

Enter police sergeant with mask and other policemen also disguised

DON MARZIO He's jail-bound for sure. Even if they discover only half of his tricks, they'll take him to prison straight-away.

SERGEANT (*to his men on the corner of the street*) Have a look around here, and when I call, come. (*his men break up*)

DON MARZIO (*aside*) Marked cards! Such thieves!

SERGEANT Coffee. (*sits down*)

TRAPPOLA At your service. (*goes for the coffee and brings it*)

SERGEANT Fine weather we're having.

DON MARZIO The weather won't last.

SERGEANT Oh well. Let's enjoy it while it's good.

DON MARZIO We won't enjoy it for long.

SERGEANT When the weather's bad, people go to a casino and gamble.

DON MARZIO You just have to go to the places where they don't rob you.

SERGEANT This gambling house nearby seems respectable.

DON MARZIO Respectable? It's a den of thieves.

SERGEANT I believe Master Pandolfo is the owner.

DON MARZIO Indeed he is.

SERGEANT To tell the truth, I've heard that he stacks the deck.

DON MARZIO He's an egregious cheat.

CAPO Ha forse truffato ancora a lei?

DON MARZIO A me no, che non son gonzo. Ma quanti capitano, tutti gli tira al trabocchetto.

CAPO Bisogna ch'egli abbia qualche timore, che non si vede.

DON MARZIO È dentro in bottega, che nasconde le carte.

CAPO Perché mai nasconde le carte?

DON MARZIO M'immagino, perché sieno fatturate.

CAPO Certamente. E dove le nasconderà?

DON MARZIO Volete ridere? Le nasconde in un ripostiglio sotto le travature.

CAPO (Ho rilevato tanto che basta). (*da sé*)

DON MARZIO Voi signore, vi dilettate di giuocare?

CAPO Qualche volta.

DON MARZIO Non mi par di conoscervi.

CAPO Or ora mi conoscerete. (*s'alza*)

DON MARZIO Andate via?

CAPO Ora torno.

TRAPPOLA Ehi! Signore, il caffè. (*al Capo*)

CAPO Or ora lo pagherò.

    (*si accosta alla strada e fischia. I birri entrano in bottega di Pandolfo*)

SCENA XII

DON MARZIO *e* TRAPPOLA

DON MARZIO (*s'alza e osserva attentamente senza parlare*)

TRAPPOLA (*anch'egli osserva attentamente*)

DON MARZIO Trappola . . .

TRAPPOLA Signor Don Marzio . . .

DON MARZIO Chi sono coloro?

TRAPPOLA Mi pare l'onorata famiglia.

SERGEANT Has he perhaps swindled you too?

DON MARZIO Not me. I'm no simpleton. But you wouldn't
believe how many he manages to lure into his trap.

SERGEANT He must be afraid of something. He's nowhere
to be found.

DON MARZIO He's inside the gambling house hiding the cards.

SERGEANT Why ever would he hide the cards?

DON MARZIO Because they've been tampered with, I imagine.

SERGEANT Of course. And where could he hide them?

DON MARZIO You want a good laugh? He hides them in a
nook under the rafters.

SERGEANT (*aside*) That's all I need to know.

DON MARZIO You, sir, do you enjoy gambling?

SERGEANT Sometimes.

DON MARZIO I don't believe I know you.

SERGEANT You'll know who I am before long. (*gets up*)

DON MARZIO Are you leaving?

SERGEANT I'll be right back.

TRAPPOLA (*to the sergeant*) Sir! Your coffee.

SERGEANT I'll pay for it in just a second.

(*the sergeant goes out to the street and whistles; his men enter
Pandolfo's gambling house.*)

SCENE XII

DON MARZIO *gets up and carefully looks around without speaking;*
TRAPPOLA *looks around carefully as well*

DON MARZIO Trappola. . . .

TRAPPOLA Signor Don Marzio. . . .

DON MARZIO Who are they?

TRAPPOLA The city's finest, I believe.

SCENA XIII

PANDOLFO *legato, birri e detti*

PANDOLFO Signor Don Marzio, gli sono obbligato.
DON MARZIO A me? Non so nulla.
PANDOLFO Io andrò forse in galera, ma la sua lingua merita
la berlina. (*va via coi birri*)
CAPO Sì signore, l'ho trovato che nascondeva le carte.
(*a Don Marzio, e parte*)
TRAPPOLA Voglio andargli dietro, per veder dove va.
(*parte*)

SCENA XIV

DON MARZIO *solo*

Oh diavolo, diavolo! Che ho io fatto? Colui, che io
credeva un signore di conto, era un birro travestito.
Mi ha tradito, mi ha ingannato. Io son di buon
cuore; dico tutto con facilità.

SCENA XV

RIDOLFO *e* LEANDRO *di casa della ballerina, e detto*

RIDOLFO Bravo; così mi piace; chi intende la ragione fa
conoscere che è uomo di garbo; finalmente in questo
mondo non abbiamo altro che il buon nome, la fama,
la riputazione. (*a Leandro*)
LEANDRO Ecco lì quello che mi ha consigliato a partire.
RIDOLFO Bravo, signor Don Marzio; ella dà di questi buoni
consigli? In vece di procurare di unirlo con la moglie, lo
persuade abbandonarla e andar via?

SCENE XIII

Enter PANDOLFO *bound at the wrists, with the sergeant's men*

PANDOLFO Signor Don Marzio, I'm obliged to you.

DON MARZIO To me? I don't know what you're talking about.

PANDOLFO Perhaps I'll be going to jail, but you and your big mouth deserve the stocks. (*exit Pandolfo with the sergeant's men*)

SERGEANT (*to Don Marzio*) Yes, sir. I caught him hiding the cards. (*exit sergeant*)

TRAPPOLA I want to follow him to see where he's going. (*exit Trappola*)

SCENE XIV

DON MARZIO Oh, what the devil! What have I done? The one I believed a reputable gentleman was a policeman in disguise. He betrayed me. He fooled me. I'm a goodhearted person—I tell everything freely.

SCENE XV

Enter RIDOLFO *and* LEANDRO *from the dancer's house*

RIDOLFO (*to Leandro*) Good man. This is more like it. He who understands reason, proves himself an admirable man. After all, the only things we have in the world are our good name, honor and reputation.

LEANDRO There he is. The one who advised me to leave.

RIDOLFO Wonderful, Signor Don Marzio. Is this your idea of advice? Instead of trying to unite him with his wife, you persuade him to abandon her and go away?

DON MARZIO Unirsi con sua moglie? È impossibile, non la vuole con lui.

RIDOLFO Per me è stato possibile; io con quattro parole l'ho persuaso. Tornerà con la moglie.

LEANDRO (Per forza, per non esser precipitato).
(*da sé*)

RIDOLFO Andiamo a ritrovar la signora Placida, che è qui dal barbiere.

DON MARZIO Andate a ritrovare quella buona razza di vostra moglie.

LEANDRO Signor Don Marzio, vi dico in confidenza, tra voi e me, che siete una gran lingua cattiva. (*entra dal barbiere con Ridolfo*)

SCENA XVI

DON MARZIO, *poi* RIDOLFO

DON MARZIO Si lamentano della mia lingua, e a me pare di parlar bene. È vero che qualche volta dico di questo e di quello, ma credendo dire la verità, non me ne astengo. Dico facilmente quello che so; ma lo faccio, perché son di buon cuore.

RIDOLFO (*dalla bottega del barbiere*) Anche questa è accomodata. Se dice davvero, è pentito. Se finge, sarà peggio per lui.

DON MARZIO Gran Ridolfo! Voi siete quello che unisce i matrimoni.

RIDOLFO Ed ella è quello che cerca di disunirli.

DON MARZIO Io ho fatto per far bene.

RIDOLFO Chi pensa male, non può mai sperar di far bene. Non s'ha mai da lusingarsi, che da una cosa cattiva ne possa derivare una buona. Separare il marito dalla moglie, è un'opera contro tutte le leggi, e non si ponno sperare che disordini e pregiudizi.

DON MARZIO Sei un gran dottore! (*con disprezzo*)

DON MARZIO Unite him with his wife? It's impossible. He
doesn't want her with him.

RIDOLFO It was possible for me. With a word or two, I
persuaded him. He'll go back to his wife.

LEANDRO (*aside*) Of course, so as not to be ruined.

RIDOLFO Let's go get Signora Placida who's waiting in
the barbershop.

DON MARZIO Go find that high-class wife of yours.

LEANDRO Signor Don Marzio, let me tell you in confidence,
between you and me, that you've got a big mouth.
(*enters the barbershop with Ridolfo*)

SCENE XVI

DON MARZIO They complain about my tongue, but it seems to
me that I speak well. It's true that sometimes I talk about
this or that. But since I tell the truth, why should I refrain
from speaking? I freely say what I know. But I do it because
I'm a goodhearted person.
(*enter Ridolfo from the barbershop*)

RIDOLFO Well, that's the end of that. If he's telling the truth,
he's repented. If he's pretending, it'll be the worse for him.

DON MARZIO The great Ridolfo! So you're the one who brings
marriages together.

RIDOLFO And you're the one who tries to take them apart.

DON MARZIO I did it to do good.

RIDOLFO He who thinks the worst, can never hope to do good.
You mustn't ever fool yourself that a good thing can derive
from a bad one. Separating a husband from his wife is a
deed against all laws, and the only things that will come
of it are misunderstanding and confusion.

DON MARZIO (*with disdain*) What a philosopher!

RIDOLFO Ella intende più di me; ma mi perdoni, la mia
lingua si regola meglio della sua.

DON MARZIO Tu parli da temerario.

RIDOLFO Mi compatisca, se vuole; e se non vuole, mi levi
la sua protezione.

DON MARZIO Te la leverò, te la leverò. Non ci verrò più a
questa tua bottega.

RIDOLFO (Oh il ciel lo volesse!) (*da sé*)

SCENA XVII

Un GARZONE *della bottega del caffè, e detti*

GARZONE Signor padrone, il signor Eugenio vi chiama.
(*si ritira*)

RIDOLFO Vengo subito; con sua licenza. (*a Don Marzio*)

DON MARZIO Riverisco il signor politico. Che cosa guadagnate
in questi vostri maneggi?

RIDOLFO Guadagno il merito di far del bene; guadagno
l'amicizia delle persone; guadagno qualche marca d'onore,
che stimo sopra tutte le cose del mondo. (*entra in bottega*)

DON MARZIO Che pazzo! Che idee da ministro, da uomo di
conto! Un caffettiere fa l'uomo di maneggio! E quanto
s'affatica! E quanto tempo vi mette! Tutte cose ch'io le avrei
accomodate in un quarto d'ora.

SCENA XVIII

RIDOLFO, EUGENIO, VITTORIA *dal caffè, e* DON MARZIO

DON MARZIO (Ecco i tre pazzi. Il pazzo discolo, la pazza gelosa,
e il pazzo glorioso). (*da sé*)

RIDOLFO In verità, provo una consolazione infinita. (*a Vittoria*)

VITTORIA Caro Ridolfo, riconosco da voi la pace, la quiete, e
posso dire la vita.

RIDOLFO You certainly understand more than I. But, pardon me, my tongue works better than yours.

DON MARZIO You speak like a reckless man.

RIDOLFO Bear with me, if you can, and if you can't, take your patronage elsewhere.

DON MARZIO I will take it elsewhere, I will. I'll never come back to this shop of yours.

RIDOLFO (*aside*) Would to God it were true!

SCENE XVII

Enter boy from the coffee house

BOY Master, Signor Eugenio is calling you. (*withdraws*)

RIDOLFO I'll be right there. (*to Don Marzio*) With your permission.

DON MARZIO My respects to the master. What do you gain from this politiking with people?

RIDOLFO I earn the merit of having done good. I earn people's friendship. I earn a mark of honor that I value above all things in the world. (*enters the shop*)

DON MARZIO What a fool! He talks like a minister or a secretary. A coffee-maker acting as a broker. And how tiring it must be! And how long it takes him! I could have taken care of everything in a quarter of an hour.

SCENE XVIII

Enter RIDOLFO, EUGENIO, *and* VITTORIA *from the coffee house*

DON MARZIO (*aside*) Here are the three fools. The mischievous fool, the jealous fool, and the glorious fool.

RIDOLFO (*to Vittoria*) In truth, this is a great blessing.

VITTORIA Dear Ridolfo, I thank you for my peace, my tranquillity, and—I can truly say—my life.

EUGENIO Credete, amico, ch'i' era stufo di far questa vita, ma
non sapeva come fare a distaccarmi dai vizi. Voi, siate
benedetto, m'avete aperto gli occhi, e un poco coi vostri
consigli, un poco coi vostri rimproveri, un poco colle
buone grazie, e un poco coi benefizi, mi avete illuminato,
mi avete fatto arrossire: sono un altr'uomo, e spero che sia
durabile il mio cambiamento, a nostra consolazione, a
gloria vostra, e ad esempio degli uomini savi, onorati e
dabbene, come voi siete.

RIDOLFO Dice troppo, signore; io non merito tanto.

VITTORIA Sino ch'io sarò viva, mi ricorderò sempre del bene
che mi avete fatto. Mi avete restituito il mio caro consorte,
l'unica cosa, che ho di bene in questo mondo. Mi ha
costato tante lagrime il prenderlo, tante me ne ha costato
il perderlo, e molte me ne costa il riacquistarlo; ma queste
sono lagrime di dolcezza, lagrime d'amore e di tenerezza,
che m'empiono l'anima di diletto, che mi fanno scordare
ogni affanno passato, rendendo grazie al cielo e lode alla
vostra pietà.

RIDOLFO Mi fa piangere dalla consolazione.

DON MARZIO (Oh pazzi maladetti!)
(*guardando sempre con l'occhialetto*)

EUGENIO Volete che andiamo a casa?

VITTORIA Mi dispiace ch'io sono ancora tutta lagrime, arruffata e
scomposta. Vi sarà mia madre e qualche altra mia parente ad
aspettarmi; non vorrei che mi vedessero col pianto agli occhi.

EUGENIO Via, achetatevi; aspettiamo un poco.

VITTORIA Ridolfo, non avete uno specchio? Vorrei un poco
vedere come sto.

DON MARZIO (Suo marito le avrà guastato il tuppé).
(*da sé, coll'occhialetto*)

RIDOLFO Se si vuol guardar nello specchio, andiamo qui sopra
nei camerini del giuoco.

EUGENIO No, là dentro non vi metto più piede.

RIDOLFO Non sa la nuova? Pandolfo è ito prigione.

EUGENIO Sì? Se lo merita; briccone! Me ne ha mangiati
tanti.

EUGENIO   Believe me, my friend, I was tired of leading that
life, but I didn't know how to break away from my
vices. You—bless your soul—have opened my eyes.
And with a little coaxing and a little criticism, with a
little charm and a little kindness, you have enlightened
me, you have humbled me. I'm a new man, and I hope
that my change will endure: here's to our blessing, to
your glory, and to the example of wise, respectable fine
men like you.

RIDOLFO   You're too kind, sir. I don't deserve it at all.

VITTORIA   As long as I live, I will remember the good that
you have done for me. You've returned to me my dear
husband, the only good thing I have in the world.
It cost me as many tears to get him as it did to lose
him. And it costs still more to get him back. But
these are tears of sweetness, tears of love and tenderness
that fill my soul with joy, that make me forget any
pain from the past. I give thanks to Heaven and praise
your mercy.

RIDOLFO   Such consolation makes me cry.

DON MARZIO   (*looking on with his lorgnette*) Accursed fools!

EUGENIO   Should we go home?

VITTORIA   I'm sorry, but I'm still all misty, messy and flustered.
My mother's probably there with some other relative of
mine waiting for me. I wouldn't want them to see me with
tears in my eyes.

EUGENIO   All right, pull yourself together. We'll wait a little.

VITTORIA   Ridolfo, do you have a mirror? I'd like to see how
I look.

DON MARZIO   (*aside, continuing to look on with the lorgnette*)
Her husband must have messed up her perruque.

RIDOLFO   If you want to use a mirror, let's go up to the rooms
above the gambling house.

EUGENIO   No, I'm not setting foot in there.

RIDOLFO   Haven't you heard the news? Pandolfo's gone to prison.

EUGENIO   Really? He deserves it. That rogue! He's raked in
plenty of my money.

VITTORIA Andiamo, caro consorte.

EUGENIO Quando non vi è nessuno, andiamo.

VITTORIA Così arruffata, non mi posso vedere.
(*entra nella bottega del giuoco con allegria*)

EUGENIO Poverina! Giubbila dalla consolazione!
(*entra, come sopra*)

RIDOLFO Vengo ancor io a servirli.
(*entra, come sopra*)

SCENA XIX

DON MARZIO, *poi* LEANDRO *e* PLACIDA

DON MARZIO Io so, perché Eugenio è tornato in pace con sua
moglie. Egli è fallito, e non ha più da vivere. La moglie è
giovane e bella . . . Non l'ha pensata male, e Ridolfo gli
farà il mezzano.

LEANDRO Andiamo dunque alla locanda, a prendere il vostro
piccolo bagaglio. (*uscendo dal barbiere*)

PLACIDA Caro marito, avete avuto tanto cuore di
abbandonarmi?

LEANDRO Via, non ne parliamo più. Vi prometto di
cambiar vita.

PLACIDA Lo voglia il cielo. (*s'avvicinano alla locanda*)

DON MARZIO Servo di vosustrissima, signor conte.
(*a Leandro burlandolo*)

LEANDRO Riverisco il signor protettore, il signor buona
lingua.

DON MARZIO M'inchino alla signora contessa.
(*a Placida deridendola*)

PLACIDA Serva, signor cavaliere delle castagne secche.
(*entra in locanda con Leandro*)

DON MARZIO Anderanno tutt'e due in pellegrinaggio a
battere la birba. Tutta la loro entrata consiste in un
mazzo di carte.

VITTORIA Let's go, my dear husband.

EUGENIO When no one's there, we'll go.

VITTORIA I'm so messy; I can't stand to see myself like this.
    (*enters the gambling house happily*)

EUGENIO Poor dear! Jubilant with bliss.
    (*enters the gambling house*)

RIDOLFO I'll come as well to serve you.
    (*enters the gambling house*)

SCENE XIX

DON MARZIO I know why Eugenio has made peace with his
    wife. He's ruined, and he hasn't anything left to live on.
    His wife is young and pretty . . . He's thought this one
    out, and Ridolfo will be his go-between.
    (*enter Leandro and Placida from the barbershop*)

LEANDRO So let's go to the inn and fetch your little baggage.

PLACIDA Dear husband, how could you have found it in your
    heart to leave me?

LEANDRO Enough. Let's not speak of it anymore. I promise you
    that I'll change my ways.

PLACIDA The Good Lord willing. (*they approach the inn*)

DON MARZIO (*to Leandro, teasing him*) Your humble servant,
    my lord, Signor Count.

LEANDRO My respects, Lord Protector, Master of the Good
    Tongue.

DON MARZIO (*to Placida, bowing, making fun of her*) I kneel
    before the Countess.

PLACIDA Your servant, Signor Knight of the Dried Chestnuts.
    (*enters the inn with Leandro*)

DON MARZIO So they'll wander about together playing their
    knavish tricks. Their whole income consists in a deck
    of cards.

SCENA XX

LISAURA *alla finestra, e* DON MARZIO

LISAURA La pellegrina è tornata alla locanda con quel
disgraziato di Leandro. S'ella ci sta troppo me ne vado
assolutamente di questa casa. Non posso tollerare la
vista né di lui, né di lei.

DON MARZIO Schiavo, signora ballerina. (*coll'occhialetto*)

LISAURA La riverisco. (*bruscamente*)

DON MARZIO Che cosa avete? Mi parete alterata.

LISAURA Mi maraviglio del locandiere, che tenga nella sua
locanda simil sorta di gente.

DON MARZIO Di chi intende parlare?

LISAURA Parlo di quella pellegrina, la quale è una donna di
mal affare, e in questi contorni non ci sono mai state di
queste porcherie.

SCENA XXI

PLACIDA *dalla finestra della locanda, e detti*

PLACIDA Eh, signorina, come parlate de' fatti miei? Io sono
una donna onorata. Non so se così si possa dire di voi.

LISAURA Se foste una donna onorata, non andreste pel
mondo birboneggiando.

DON MARZIO (*ascolta e osserva di qua e di là coll'occhialetto,
e ride*)

PLACIDA Sono venuta in traccia di mio marito.

LISAURA Sì, e l'anno passato in traccia di chi eravate?

PLACIDA Io a Venezia non ci sono più stata.

LISAURA Siete una bugiarda. L'anno passato avete fatta una
trista figura in questa città. (*Don Marzio osserva, e ride
come sopra*)

PLACIDA Chi v'ha detto questo?

LISAURA Eccolo lì; il signor Don Marzio me l'ha detto.

SCENE XX

Enter LISAURA *at the window*

LISAURA The wayfarer's gone back to the inn with that
no-good Leandro. If she's there too long, I'm leaving
this house for good. I can't tolerate the sight of either
of them.
DON MARZIO (*with his lorgnette*) Your servant, Signora
Ballerina.
LISAURA (*brusquely*) My respects.
DON MARZIO What's wrong? You seem upset.
LISAURA I'm amazed that the innkeeper takes such people
at his inn.
DON MARZIO Who do you mean?
LISAURA I mean that wayfarer, the tart. We've never had
such riff-raff in our neighborhood.

SCENE XXI

Enter PLACIDA *at the window of the inn*

PLACIDA Signorina, what are you saying about me? I'm a
respectable woman. I'm not sure I can say the same for you.
LISAURA If you were a respectable woman, you wouldn't go
around the world playing knavish tricks on people.
DON MARZIO (*listens and looks on now and then with his
lorgnette and laughs*)
PLACIDA I came in search of my husband.
LISAURA Really. And last year, who were you in search of?
PLACIDA I have never been to Venice before.
LISAURA You're a liar. Last year you cut a rather bad figure
in this city. (*Don Marzio looks on with his lorgnette
and laughs*)
PLACIDA Who told you that?
LISAURA There he is. Signor Don Marzio told me.

DON MARZIO Io non ho detto nulla.

PLACIDA Egli non può aver detto una tal bugia; ma di voi sì, mi ha narrata la vita e i bei costumi. Mi ha egli informata dell'esser vostro, e che ricevete le genti di nascosto per la porta di dietro.

DON MARZIO Io non l'ho detto. (*sempre coll'occhialetto di qua e di là*)

PLACIDA Sì, che l'avete detto.

LISAURA È possibile che il signor Don Marzio abbia detto di me una simile iniquità?

DON MARZIO Vi dico, non l'ho detto.

SCENA XXII

EUGENIO *alla finestra de' camerini, poi* RIDOLFO *da altra simile, poi* VITTORIA *dall'altra, aprendole di mano in mano, e detti a' loro luoghi*

EUGENIO Sì, che l'ha detto, e l'ha detto anche a me, e dell'una, e dell'altra. Della pellegrina, che è stata l'anno passato a Venezia a birboneggiare, e della signora ballerina, che riceve le visite per la porta di dietro.

DON MARZIO Io l'ho sentito dir da Ridolfo.

RIDOLFO Io non son capace di dir queste cose. Abbiamo anzi altercato per questo. Io sosteneva l'onore della signora Lisaura, e V.S. voleva che fosse una donna cattiva.

LISAURA Oh disgraziato!

DON MARZIO Sei un bugiardo.

VITTORIA A me ancora ha detto che mio marito teneva pratica colla ballerina e colla pellegrina; e me l'ha dipinte per due scelleratissime femmine.

PLACIDA Ah scellerato!

LISAURA Ah maladetto!

DON MARZIO I didn't say anything.

PLACIDA He couldn't have told such a lie. But he did tell me about your life and fine manners. He informed me about your ways, and he told me that you secretly receive people through the back door.

DON MARZIO (*continues to look on with his lorgnette*) I didn't say that.

PLACIDA You did too.

LISAURA Is it possible that Signor Don Marzio said such bad things about me?

DON MARZIO I'm telling you that I didn't say that.

SCENE XXII

Enter EUGENIO *at a window of the gambling house*

EUGENIO He did too, and he said it to me as well, about each of them: the wayfarer was in Venice last year playing knavish tricks, and the dancer receives visitors through the back door.

DON MARZIO I heard it from Ridolfo. (*Enter Ridolfo, opening a window*)

RIDOLFO I wouldn't dream of saying such a thing. Just the opposite: we argued over this. I defended Signora Lisaura's honor, and you, good sir, held that she was a bad woman.

LISAURA You wretch!

DON MARZIO You're a liar. (*Enter Vitoria, opening a window*)

VITTORIA And he told me that my husband was intimate with both the dancer and the wayfarer. He portrayed them as two very wicked women.

PLACIDA Oh, you wicked man!

LISAURA Accursed one!

SCENA XXIII

LEANDRO *sulla porta della locanda, e detti*

LEANDRO Signor sì, signor sì, V.S. ha fatto nascere mille disordini; ha levata la riputazione colla sua lingua a due donne onorate.

DON MARZIO Anche la ballerina onorata?

LISAURA Tale mi vanto di essere. L'amicizia col signor Leandro non era che diretta a sposarlo, non sapendo che egli avesse altra moglie.

PLACIDA La moglie l'ha, e sono io quella.

LEANDRO E se avessi abbadato al signor Don Marzio, l'avrei nuovamente sfuggita.

PLACIDA Indegno!

LISAURA Impostore!

VITTORIA Maldicente!

EUGENIO Ciarlone!

DON MARZIO A me questo? A me, che sono l'uomo il più onorato del mondo?

RIDOLFO Per essere onorato non basta non rubare, ma bisogna anche trattar bene.

DON MARZIO Io non ho mai commessa una mala azione.

SCENA XXIV

TRAPPOLA, *e detti*

TRAPPOLA Il signor Don Marzio l'ha fatta bella.

RIDOLFO Che ha fatto?

TRAPPOLA Ha fatto la spia a messer Pandolfo, l'hanno legato, e si dice che domani lo frusteranno.

RIDOLFO È uno spione! Via dalla mia bottega.
    (*parte dalla finestra*)

SCENE XXIII

Enter LEANDRO *at the door of the inn*

LEANDRO Yes sir, yes sir. You, my good sir, gave rise to a
thousand misunderstandings. With that tongue of yours
you ruined the reputation of two respectable ladies.

DON MARZIO You think the dancer's respectable?

LISAURA Respectable and proud of it. My friendship
with Signor Leandro was directed toward nothing
less than marriage with him—not knowing that he
had a wife.

PLACIDA A wife he has, and it's me.

LEANDRO And if I had done what Signor Don Marzio said,
I would have fled from her again.

PLACIDA You despicable man!

LISAURA Impostor!

VITTORIA Scandalmonger!

EUGENIO Blabber!

DON MARZIO Me? Me, the most respectable man in the world?

RIDOLFO To be respectable, its not enough not to steal. You
have to be kind as well.

DON MARZIO I have never done a bad deed.

SCENE XXIV

Enter TRAPPOLA

TRAPPOLA Signor Don Marzio's done it this time.

RIDOLFO What did he do?

TRAPPOLA He betrayed Master Pandolfo's confidence. They
tied him up, and they say that tomorrow they're going
to whip him.

RIDOLFO He's an informer! Get out of my shop.
(*leaves the window*)

SCENA XXV

Il GARZONE *del barbiere, e detti*

GARZONE Signore spione, non venga più a farsi fare la barba
nella nostra bottega.
(entra nella sua bottega)

SCENA ULTIMA

Il CAMERIERE *della locanda, e detti*

CAMERIERE Signora spia, non venga più a far desinari alla
nostra locanda. *(entra nella locanda)*
LEANDRO Signor protettore; tra voi e me in confidenza:
far la spia è azion da briccone.
(entra nella locanda)
PLACIDA Altro, che castagne secche! Signor soffione.
(parte dalla finestra)
LISAURA Alla berlina, alla berlina.
(parte dalla finestra)
VITTORIA O che caro signor Don Marzio! Quei dieci zecchini,
che ha prestati a mio marito, saranno stati una paga di
esploratore. *(parte dalla finestra)*
EUGENIO Riverisco, il signor confidente.
(parte dalla finestra)
TRAPPOLA Io fo riverenza al signor referendario.
(entra in bottega)
DON MARZIO Sono stordito, sono avvilito, non so in qual
mondo mi sia. Spione a me? A me spione? Per avere svelato
accidentalmente il reo costume di Pandolfo, sarò imputato
di spione? Io non conosceva il birro, non prevedeva
l'inganno, non sono reo di questo infame delitto. Eppur
tutti m'insultano, tutti mi vilipendono, niuno mi vuole,
ognuno mi scaccia. Ah sì, hanno ragione, la mia lingua, o

SCENE XXV

Enter barber's BOY

BOY Signor Squealer, don't come to our shop anymore for
a shave.
(*enters his shop*)

SCENE LAST

Enter WAITER

WAITER Signor Squealer, don't come to our inn anymore for
dinner. (*enters the inn*)
LEANDRO Signor Protector, between you and me, in
confidence, such a betrayal is the act of a rogue.
(*enters the inn*)
PLACIDA You and your dried chestnuts! Signor Tattletale.
(*leaves the window*)
LISAURA Put him in the stocks, in the stocks.
(*leaves the window*)
VITTORIA Oh, what a dear you are Signor Don Marzio! You
were probably using those ten sequins that you lent my
husband as a bribe for information. (*leaves the window*)
EUGENIO My respects to Signor Informer.
(*leaves the window*)
TRAPPOLA I kneel to the Reverend Signor Referendary.
(*enters the shop*)
DON MARZIO I'm overwhelmed. I'm a broken man. What kind
of world is this? Me, an informer? An informer? I'm
accused of being a tattletale just for having accidentally
revealed Pandolfo's evil ways? I didn't know the policeman.
I didn't foresee his trickery. I'm not guilty of such a
despicable crime. And yet they all insult me. They all

presto, o tardi, mi doveva condurre a qualche gran precipizio. Ella mi ha acquistata l'infamia, che è il peggiore de' mali. Qui non serve il giustificarmi. Ho perduto il credito e non lo riacquisto mai più. Anderò via di questa città; partirò a mio dispetto, e per causa della mia trista lingua mi priverò d'un paese, in cui tutti vivono bene, tutti godono la libertà, la pace, il divertimento; quando sanno essere prudenti, cauti ed onorati. (*parte*)

slander me. Nobody wants me. Everyone chases me away. Oh, I guess they're right. My loose tongue had to lead me to this fall, sooner or later. It's brought me disgrace, something worse than any ill. There's no excuse. I've lost my good name and I'll never get it back again. I'll leave this city. I'll leave in spite of myself, and because of this awful tongue of mine, I'll give up a city where all live well, all have freedom, peace, and joy as long as they know how to be cautious, careful and honorable.
(*exit Don Marzio*)

NOTES

1. Lorenzo Da Ponte, *Memorie*, ed Giovanni Gambarin and Fausto Nicolini, Bari: Laterza, 1918, I, p. 218: "go to London, but when you are there, never go to the *Café of Italians*"; and further, on Da Ponte's comment: "Almost all of my troubles and losses that I suffered in that city came from my frequenting the *Café of Italians* . . ." (Translations from the Italian and French are mine, unless otherwise specified.)
2. *Paris le jour, Paris la nuit:* Louis Sébastien Mercier, *Tableau de Paris, Le Nouveau Paris*. Restif de la Bretonne, *Les Nuits de Paris*, ed. Daniel Baruch, Paris: Laffont, 1990, pp. 69-70.
3. *The Spectator*, ed. Donald F. Bond, Oxford: Clarendon Press, 1965, 5 vols. This material referenced by issue number of the serial *The Spectator*.
4. *Lettres persanes*, XXXIV, ed. Paul Vernière, Paris: Garnier, 1960, pp. 77-78.
5. Gasparo Gozzi, *L'Osservatiore Veneto*, LVIII, ed. Emilio Spagni, Florence: barbera, 1914, pp. 241-242.
6. *"Il Caffè" 1764-1766*, eds. Gianni Francioni and Sergio Romagnoli, Turin: Boringhieri, 1993, p. 12.
7. *Mémoires*, II, 7: *Tutte le opere*, ed. Giuseppe Ortolani, Milan: Mondadori, 1935-56, 14 vols., I. p. 271.
8. This is the thesis of Ted Emery, "'Da La bottega da caffè' a 'La bottega del caffè': le contraddizioni del mercato e la riforma goldoniana," in *Sudi Goldoniani* 7 (1985), pp. 46-59. By the same author, see also: *Goldoni as Librettist. Theatrical Reform and the "Drammi Giocosi per Musica,"* New York: Peter Lang, 1991, pp. 46-55.
9. See Milena Montanile, "Struttura comica e morale economica nella "Bottega del caffè" di Carlo Goldoni," in *Esperienze letterarie*, VIII, 1 (1983), pp. 31-49. With regard to the relationship between our text and the commedia dell'arte, we should not forget that in the 1750 performances, the role of the coffee-house owner, which became Ridolfo in the printed version, was still played by Brighella (see "The Author to the Reader." For some instances that bring us back to the tradition of the old Italian Comedy, one can think of Don Marzio coming out of the barber shop with a towel around his neck and lather on his face (I); Placida disguised as a traveller (I); the duel

between Leandro and Eugenio (II); or Eugenio threatening his own wife with his sword (II).

10. Ilaria Crotti, "Il mondo niovo del caffè," *Annali d'Italianistica*, 11 (1993): *Goldoni 1993*, pp. 139-58 (for the passages quoted, see pp. 146-52).

11. Jackson I. Cope, "Honor among the Denizens of Goldoni's 'botteghe da caffè,'" ibid., pp. 159-72 (passage quoted, p. 171).

12. Carlo Goldoni, "La bottega del caffè," ed. Roberta Turchi, Venice: Marsilio, 1994, "Introduzione," pp. 9-24.

13. Eugenio Levi, *Il comico di carattere da Teofrasto a Pirandello*, Turin: Einaudi, 1959, pp. 115-25.

14. Mario Baratto, "Le café et le théâtre de Goldoni" (1962), in *La letteratura teatrale del Settecento in Italia (Studi e letture su Carlo Goldoni)*, Vicenza: Neri Pozza, 1985, pp. 61-75.

15. Jacques Joly, "Il luogo scenico del 'campiello' nelle commedie del Goldoni," *Problemi*, May-August 1974, pp. 116-41 (passage quoted, p. 123).

16. Carlo Goldoni, *The Holiday Trilogy*, trans. Anthony Oldcorn, New York: Marsilio Publishers, 1994, p. 97.

17. My remarks on the horizontal and vertical movements to which the action of the comedy obeys were in part suggested by the essays of Jacques Joly and Roberta Turchi quoted above (nn. 15 and 12, respectively), to which I am glad to acknowledge my debt.

18. It is very likely that Goldoni knew "Le Médisant" of Philippe Néricault Destouches (1715) and "Le Méchant" of Jean Baptiste Louis Gresset (1745). But his Don Marzio doesn't owe anything to them. On the contrary, several traits in the character and behavior of Eugenio were clearly sugegsted to Goldoni by Valère, the protagonist of "Le Joueur" by Jean François Regnard (1696).

19. In any case, we must credit Goldoni with having brought for the first time into Italian theater and literature the coffee house, "one of the most typical gathering places in the eighteenth century" (R. Turchi, "Introduzione," quoted. p. 12).

20. For the social type of the young jolly sportsman Eugenio tries— without much success—to resemble, see Goldoni's *Mémoires*, I, 40: "The true Venetian *cortesan* is serviceable, officious, and possessed of probity. He is generous without profusion; gay without rashness; fond of women without involving himself; fond of pleasure without ruining himself; he is prepared to bear a part in everything for the good of society; he prefers tranquillity, but will not allow himself to be duped; he is affable to all, a warm friend, and a zealous protector. Is not this an accomplished man?" (*Memoirs*

of Carlo Goldoni Written by Himself, trans. John Black, ed. William A. Drake, New York: Knopf, 1954; reprint: Westport, Conn.: Greenwood Press, 1976, here p. 182); and also Carlo Gozzi, *Memorie inutili,* I, 17: ". . . a certain kind of people, called in Venice *cortigiani* were shopkeepers, artisans, not without some priests, men of parts, honorable, well acquainted with the world of Venice, brave, respected by the populace for their courage, their interposing between fighters, and because they know how to enjoy themselves a lot spending a little" (ed. Giuseppe Prezzolini, Bari: Laterza, 1910, p. 113).

The Text
"The Coffee House" was first published in 1753 by Bettinelli (Le Commedie, Venice, vol. IV), without the author's consent. It was reprinted soon thereafter by Paperini (Le Commedie, Florence, 1753, vol. I), revised by Goldoni, and much later—after numerous other, less reliable printings—in the magnificient Pasquali edition (*Commedie,* Venice, 1761, vol. I), also supervised by the author.

The text of the present edition which itself that of Roberta Turchi (Venice: Marsilio 1994) is based on the Pasquali and Paperini editions.

The Coffee House on stage
Our play was staged for the first time on May 2nd, 1750 in Mantua, by the Medebach Company, and the following fall and early winter in Venice at the Sant'Angelo Theater, with considerable success (at least a dozen performances).

It became immediately popular, and from the late eighteenth century to this day has remained in the repertoires of major Italian troupes, often under the alternative title "Il maldicente" ("The Backbiter," or "The Scandalmonger"). Another mark of its popularity is to be seen in the numerous *libretti per musica* it inspired, and in the proven or probable influence it exerted on other distinguished playwrights, such as Voltaire ("L'Ecossaise," 1760) and Lessing ("Minna von Barnhelm," 1766-77). A recent and significant instance of "The Coffee House's" appeal was the revision into German of "Das Kaffeehaus," written and staged by Peter Raben and Reiner Werner Fassbinder (September 10, 1969, Theater der Freien Hansestadt in Bremen).

The fact that *The Coffee House* is still successfully performed is the best proof that, in the actors' and directors' opinion, its theatrical qualities largely compensate for the play's eventual weaknesses. Some of these qualities, as suggested in the Introduction, have to do with the liveliness of the open-air action, the natural sound of the dialogue, and the possibilities the character of Don Marzio offers to skillful interpreters.

The American reception
In the near-desert of American interest in Goldoni's theater, "The Coffee House" has been relatively lucky. The first scenes of Act I were included by C.D. Werner in his vast anthology *Library of the World's Best Literature* (New York, 1897, vol. XI), and a complete translation was published some thirty years later under the title "The Coffee House" (trans. Henry B. Fuller, New York: S. French Publ., 1925).

More interestingly, Fuller's translation was staged, and of that performance and its reception we give the account left by the best American biographer of Goldoni to this day, H.C. Chatfield-Taylor:

Translated into English by Mr. Henry B. Fuller, this comedy was presented by The Drama Players, under the auspices of the Chicago Theatre Society, during the dramatic season of 1912, and received with mild curiosity, not to say indifference, by an American audience; yet in extenuation of this ill success, it may be said that the actors, temperamentally unsuited to their parts, had been insufficiently rehearsed, and that the play had been hurriedly staged without having received the judicious pruning so necessary to a modern revival of old comedy. Although one Chicago critic declared that "*The Coffee House* will inspire no emotion save that of ennui," while another dismissed it as "artistic fluff," the charm of this quaintly naturalistic comedy was keenly felt by that intrepid champion of dramatic excellence, Mr. James O'Donnell Bennett, of the *Record-Herald*, his critique being so intuitively just to this droll portrayal of the life of Venice in her decadence that it shall be quoted here as a vicarious expression of the present writer's views regarding that quaint fabric of naïveté sapiency. *The Coffee House*, was enacted, probably for the first time on the English speaking stage, at the Lyric Theatre last evening before an assemblage that at first seemed to be rubbing its eyes to adjust its vision to a composition that, when you have adjusted yourself to it, is very engaging. When the audience had put itself back into Venice of the mid-eighteenth century, and when it began to sense the kindliness, the homely wisdom, the sweet trustfulness and the soft drollery that distinguish everything the good Carlo Goldoni wrote—then it enjoyed itself. Until then it seemed dissatisfied—wondering perhaps with what relic the Chicago Theatre Society was trying to fool it.

But you cannot long resist "Dr. Goldoni, a Venetian lawyer," as they called him in the early days of his memorable career. . . . He is one of the loves of literature, and it was a genuine pleasure to this reviewer to sit with him last evening and observe him in his kindly, busy, deft, officious, sometimes artless and sometimes very shrewd way, manœuvering the people he knew so thoroughly in that trivial, impetuous, genial Venice of his.

Here came the male babbler, preening and mincing in lace and silk, sipping his coffee in the open, lying in wait for a bit of gossip like a cat for a mouse, putting two and two together and making what he liked out of it, symbolizing—in a different way but just as wonderfully—the "motiveless malignity" of Iago, and epitomizing mischief and malevolence. . . . The character is drawn full length—perfect in every puttering detail, an officious, gloating, eavesdropping babbler who wins for himself in the denouement the word—of terrifying import in the Venice of 1760—"spy," and who thinks himself so little deserving of that word that he whimpers as the curtain falls: "I have a good heart, but—but—I talk too much!" He is an unforgivable, unforgettable old man, and he was as alive last night as he was one hundred and fifty-two years ago.

Here is that Signor Eugenio, who "pursues women and gambles like a madman"; here the old servant of the father of Eugenio, who has saved his money and opened a coffee-house and declares with honest pride that his is a calling which, when pursued aright, serves alike the pleasure and the comfort of the town; here the gambler and his gulls; here neglected wives voicing their griefs with the gorgeous virulence characteristic of their race; here the impudent servants who know too much. They are all alive. Babbler, crook, spendthrift, benevolent old man, the acquisitive and the inquisitive—they go busily their ways. Innuendo, protest, impeachment, denial fly through the air. The old servant reconciles the contentious, heartens up the grieving, assists the penniless, tries to implant good sense and right feeling in the soul of even the crooked gambler, reunites estranged husbands and wives, brings everything to a happy issue for everybody,—except the mean scandalmonger. Him the sunny Carlo cannot forgive, and at the end he sends him trailing across a deserted stage, the hateful word "spy"—informer would perhaps convey the meaning better—ringing in his ears.

The mechanism of it has occasionally been so obvious that in these knowing days a child could run it. Sometimes the movement has been forced and tame. But the human nature of it is valid. We know that these people existed, that they hurried and idled and gossiped and quarrelled in yonder sunlit square, irascible, volatile, weal, venomous, distracted. They rejoiced. They suffered. They lived.

[Goldoni: A Biography. (New York: Duffield & Co., 1913. 285-87.]

Bibliography
Essential reading for anyone wishing to find out more about Goldoni and his works are his *Mémoires pour servir à l'histoire de sa vie et à celle de son théâtre*, written in French and published in Paris (chez la veuve Duchesne) in 1787 in three volumes, and translated into English by John Black (London, 1814). The English translation was twice reprinted-by Alfred Knopf (New York, 1926) and by the Greenwood Press (Westport, Connecticut, 1976) edited, with an Introduction, by William A. Drake.

Among the scant works available on Goldoni in English, the only really useful contributions are the out-of-print volumes by H. C. Chatfield-Taylor, *Goldoni. A Biography* (New York: Duffield and Co., 1913) and Joseph Spencer Kennard, *Goldoni and the Venice of His Time* (New York The Macmillan Co., 1920). Considerably less reliable are the more recent: Heinz Riedt, *Carlo Goldoni*, translated from the German by Ursule Molinaro (New York: F. Ungar, 1974); Linda L. Carroll, *Language and Dialect in Ruzante and Goldoni* (Ravenna: Longo Editore, 1981); and Eugene Steele, *Carlo Goldoni. Life, Work, and Times* (Ravenna: Longo Editore, 1981). Preferable to these, and profusely illustrated, is Timothy Holme, *A Servant of Many Masters The Life and Times of Carlo Goldoni* (London: Jupiter, 1976)

On *The Coffee House* in particular, see the essays already quoted in our "Introduction": Ted Emery, *Goldoni as Librettist. Theatrical Reform and the 'Drammi giocosi per musica,'* New York: Peter Lang, 1991, pp. 46-55; and Jackson I. Cope, "Honor among the Denizens of Goldoni's *"botteghe da caffè,"* *Annali D'Italianistica*, 11 (1993): *Goldoni 1993*, pp. 139-58.

For the secondary literature in Italian, French, German, etc., see: Nicola Mangini, *Bibliografia goldoniana 1908-1957*, Venezia-Roma: Istituto per la Collaborazione Culturale, 1961, with the *Supplementi* by the same Mangini published in the eight issues of *Studi goldoniani*, Venezia, 1968 1988; and the "Bibliografia" appended by R. Turchi to her edition of *La bottega del caffè*, quoted, pp. 245-49.

MARSILIO CLASSICS

Amerigo Vespucci, *Letters From A New World*
Edited by Luciano Formisano. Foreword by Garry Wills

Denis Diderot, *The Indiscreet Jewels*
Introduction by Aram Vartanian

Jacques Cazotte, *The Devil in Love*
Followed by Nerval's *Life of Cazotte*

Carlo Goldoni, *The Holiday Trilogy*
Introduction by Franco Fido

Lauro Martines, *An Italian Renaissance Sextet*
Six Tales in Historical Context

Heinrich Heine, *The Harz Journey*
Foreword by Claudio Magris

Heinrich Heine, *Journey to Italy*
A New Edition by Christopher Johnson

Antonio Pigafetta, *The First Voyage Around the World*
Edited by Ted Cachey

Ralph Waldo Emerson, *Representative Men*
Edited by Pamela Schirmeister

Cesare Beccaria, *Of Crimes and Punishments*
Foreword by Mario Cuomo.
Introduction by Marvin Wolfgang

Luigi Ballerini and Andrew Wood
Series Editors

Printed in the United States
40915LVS00002B/76-78